God's Call

Clive Gerrard

Marabou Editions Ltd.

Kampala, Uganda

ISBN-10-9970494015
ISBN-13-9789970494019

DEDICATION

To SHANNY

Many years ago, after I had just become a Christian, I was very fortunate to have a Minister who had a special relationship with Jesus. Her love for Jesus and for His Word came across when she taught; she was very inspiring to all who heard her speak. Even though she is no longer with us I will always be indebted to her for passing on her passion for God's Word to me; it's really through her and the notes I jotted down that this book has been written. I am hoping to pass on this passion to others as they read this book and delve into God's Word for themselves.

I would also like to thank our very good friends Owen and Lavinia for enabling this book to be published. Without their love and support this book would probably have remained on the drawing table, but with Owen's expertise and his knowledge of publishing this book has become a reality.

Finally, I would like to say a BIG thank you to my wife Shanny for her constant support in all that I do.

CONTENTS

i

Chapter 1: God's call

Since the dawn of time man's inquisitive nature has led him down the path of self-discovery. This nature quickly helped man to conquer not only his surrounding environment but has also enabled him to investigate areas that once seemed out of his reach. In the 21st century, as man's knowledge has quickly grown, we are using modern technology and improvements in science to investigate and break down what we assume are the final barriers that explain our existence. Every boundary is being pushed back as we attempt to become the masters of our universe.

In the last 20 years man could not have imagined that technology would have developed so fast. But it's not only the sciences that have shown improvement. It's actually every area of our lives, from living conditions to education, from medicine to computers. Our understanding of the world in which we live has grown immensely. Yet for some reason, even in the face of all these modern developments, the world is still full of intrigue and mysteries. In the natural world we apparently know more about space than we do about the depths of the oceans. It's thought that there are many creatures in the sea still waiting to be discovered. As we look back in time, the debate about who built the pyramids rages on. How did they move those huge stones? How were they able to build those structures with such accuracy? This is also true when people look at Stonehenge. Even with our technology it's hard to comprehend how all this was achieved. There are also areas in the world where strange phenomena occur on a regular basis. Areas such as the Bermuda Triangle and the Dragon's Triangle are associated with the disappearance of many planes and ships. These areas as well as many others are also associated with UFO sightings. There are also legends about King Arthur, Atlantis, Big Foot and many more that may or may not be true. They have all been investigated but for now the true explanations are hidden away from view.

The scriptures of the Bible are also full of mysteries. They tell us we were created by God. They speak of angels and serpents that talk. They tell us that seas were parted and water sprung forth out of rocks. They speak of people such as Elijah and Elisha who brought fire down from the sky. We have stories about Ezekiel's visions, chariots appearing out of the blue to take Elijah up into the heavens. We have stories that tell of God's invisible armies surrounding the enemy, and we are told of Daniel who was placed in a lion's den but came out of it unscathed. The New Testament speaks of a man who performed miracles, who walked on water and turned water into wine. He also raised the dead and His followers also healed people after He himself was raised from the dead. We have all these mysteries and many more in one book. They are fascinating and capture our imagination as much as the mysteries mentioned earlier.

Modern technology is not only used by scientists to uncover the mysteries of the universe. It's also used by archaeologists to throw new light on many of the stories in the Bible. For some it's a chance to disprove that God exists. For others it gives them the opportunity to prove that these characters really walked this earth. Both sides analyse each tiny clue as they are unearthed. They study and date each artefact hoping that one day their findings will be the piece in their jigsaw that unlocks the Bible's secrets for good or for bad depending on their personal belief.

The biased opinions by both sides only bring about confusion. People are unsure who to believe. Do they put their trust in evidence that is put forward by scientists, or do they believe the Christian viewpoint that they should walk in faith? The best way forward is to search through the evidence yourselves, take on board what everyone is saying and then make an informed decision.

I have always been fascinated by both arguments. I would be glued to the TV when scientific program weas being shown or programs that investigated the paranormal. Similarly, this was true when films about Jesus were televised. I would pretend that I wasn't bothered but secretly I was always intrigued. Later on in my life I made the choice to become a Christian. I didn't really know a lot about the Bible. I had heard stories from the Old Testament and of course I knew about Jesus. It was only when someone told me that Jesus wanted to be a part of my life that I knew deep down that choosing for God was the right thing to do. I look at the scientific evidence and I always relate it to God. I use the visible to picture the invisible. Through God's Word I now believe that God is in all things. He is the artist that has painted creation.

The scriptures of the Bible are themselves like little clues. If we look at them closely and study their meaning, they can unlock the mysteries of the universe. But, more importantly for us, they can unlock the answers to the questions that we have all been asking i.e. 'What is the purpose to life?', 'Why is there suffering in the world?', 'What happens when we die?' God's Word is fantastic. The scriptures allow us to enter into spiritual realms that we know nothing about. They explain how creation came into being. For those who look deep enough the scriptures show us that the world did not just happen by chance. They inform us that there is a God and He has a master plan. The Word of God will show us that this plan involves us; each and every one of us. It may seem to us that this plan isn't working at the moment because of all the chaos in the world, but God's plan is precise. He has told us that all this chaos is going to happen. He has also given us the key that will allow us to escape it. To be a part of this plan the scriptures tell us that we have to accept Jesus Christ as Saviour, to accept that He died in our place upon the cross. So all the tiny clues are there for us to dig down deep and look. We have all the answers to the above questions before our eyes. We just have to be willing, like archaeologists, to spend time searching for the answers.

There is a verse in the Bible that says that God has chosen us, we did not choose him (John 15v16) and I know this is true in my own life. Many years ago, when I was still at school, we had a new RE teacher who wasn't anything special. Compared to our last RE teacher he seemed a bit of a pushover, yet it was through him that I became a Christian. Although I didn't realise it at the time, God had chosen me. Why? I don't know! But He had, and looking back now I suppose I can see his hand guiding me in the right direction.

From an early age I always said my prayers. I don't know why, but I did. I just felt that it was right to ask God to keep my family and me safe. I now believe that He did. Without really understanding who God was when I was younger, I remember that the stories of the Bible were constantly in my ear e.g. there was a time when I was in the Infants' school when one of the teachers told a story about a man who remained silent when he was being accused of something that he hadn't done. I remember how this story fascinated me. I was quite the opposite. I was always being accused of things that I *had* done, but I always denied that it was me. Hearing this story made me want to change. I thought to myself the next time that I was accused I would say nothing, but it never happened. I continued to get into trouble and I always had an excuse. I remember an incident when I was running across the road chasing my friend. I remember watching, in slow-motion, as a car nearly hit me. Maybe the car wasn't travelling very fast at all. Maybe the whole scenario was very different to anyone who was watching. But the incident stuck in my mind and it gave me the feeling that someone was watching over me.

After this near miss I can't recall any other major incidents. My life was probably like everybody else's. I grew up in a fairly rough area. To survive or fit in you had to be tough, or at least pretend to be tough. If you weren't then life could be hard. There wasn't much to do back then. We had a youth club but most of the time we spent our nights on street corners or, if we were lucky, someone's parents would go out and we would all end up there for the evening.

When I was about 15 years old the Gospel Bus came to our area. It was a double-decker bus that was run by a group of Christians who were spreading the good news of Jesus. We could go on the bus and have a chat and a cup of tea. I can't really say this influenced me, but on some level it must have played its part. The seeds were being sown and I didn't even realise it. God had called me and the way was being made clear for me to answer that call.

The incident that probably changed the way I thought about God occurred one day when I was at school. One day in an RE lesson the teacher said he was going to show us a video. He explained that this video was about the rapture ('the rapture' means the end of times i.e. when God returns to His creation). He said that he believed that this was going to actually happen one day. We all watched the video in silence. I can't remember if we discussed the video, but I do know that it had affected me on some deep level. As a known troublemaker in the school, I didn't let on to anybody about how the video had affected me. But I remember that same night I had a talk with God. Well, I talked and hoped that if there was a God that He was listening. I explained to Him that I believed that the video was true, but at this present time I couldn't do anything about it. I couldn't follow Him yet, because of all the abuse that I would get off my friends. I put an emphasis on the 'yet' part and I asked the Lord not to forget me. Then I went to sleep and the next day I carried on as normal, as if nothing had happened.

Just before I left school, we used to play around with Ouija boards. It always seemed as if someone was moving the glass but we were never really sure, and we often didn't stay to find out. One of the girls pretended that she was possessed. It was all taken light-heartedly but when I went home I found it difficult to fall asleep. I would be always looking around the room to see if anything was there. We went to a church about it and the minister talked to her and gave us all some Jesus stickers. When I returned home I put these stickers on my headboard. That night I had no problem sleeping. These stickers actually gave me great comfort and made me feel safe. Nothing really changed after these events. I left school early without taking any exams, went to work, played football and went to the pub with the lads. For someone looking from the outside they would say that I had a good life.

My life began to change one day when I was playing football. I was playing in one of the biggest cup finals in Staffordshire. It was the President's Cup. It had taken a lot of hard work to get to this final; it was the pinnacle of our season. We drew the first match, so the game had to be replayed and we won 3-2. I scored one of the goals, so you would think that I would be on a high. Instead, when I received my trophy, the only thing that I could think was 'is that it?' What a let-down! After all the hard work of getting into the final, it was over and I felt so deflated. We celebrated our victory that night, we all got drunk and these thoughts were quickly forgotten. I went home that night in a good mood with my trophy proudly on display.

It was one night when I was out with my friends that

these thoughts and feelings returned. We were in our local pub enjoying a beer. We were all having a good time, when I suddenly thought 'is this all there is to life?' Although I never told anyone, I kept having the same thoughts and feelings. It wasn't long after this that the Lord finally revealed Himself to me. I was at work and it seemed to be just a normal day. As we were working and talking one of my colleagues told me that he had gone to a church meeting the night before. His words intrigued me and deep down I knew that what he was saying was right. We carried on discussing the subject all day. He invited me to the next meeting which was later on that day. I can't remember what was said in the meeting but that same night I asked Christ into my life. The most amazing thing came into my mind when I was asking the Lord into my life. He reminded me of the 'yet' that I had mentioned when I was younger. He was telling me that he had not forgotten what I had said.

Although I may have been living my life the way I wanted to, God was using every situation to show me that life was meaningless without him in it. He had brought me to this point in my life where He was giving me another chance to answer His call. I still could have said no, the time is still not right. I could have made numerous excuses not to follow Him, but I said yes, and it is the best decision that I have ever made. God gives us all the choice to either say yes or no. He has given us all free will. He will never force Himself on us; it has got to be our decision.

Although it was the best decision that I have ever made, it was also the hardest. Not physically, but emotionally and mentally. To say yes to Christ meant that I was going to have to turn my back on the life that I was leading. I no longer felt that it was right to go to nightclubs. I felt, rightly or wrongly, that my nights of drinking were now over. As a new Christian I didn't really know what God expected from me. I didn't know His principles so I gave up nearly everything. Deep down I knew my choices were right for me at that time and I braced myself for the consequences. I lost a lot of close friends who didn't understand what was going on. They thought that I had gone mad, but through all the turmoil that my decision had created I began to find my true self and I gradually turned my back on the old life that I used to live.

My life was turned upside down, but I gradually began to mature spiritually. I began to understand

what it means to be a Christian in today's world. My preconceived ideas of what a Christian should be like were quickly shattered. I was taught early on that although I am now saved from all my sins, I still have an old nature within me that still wants to act contrary to God's will. The analogy we used to describe this nature was from the scriptures in Exodus. Pharaoh is an excellent description of our old nature. He built treasure cities to show his own importance. His pride wanted everyone to know who he was. Pharaoh reflects our old nature exactly because he represents the side of us in our unconscious that only wants to live for self.

This struggle between the old and new natures is revealed throughout the Bible. It's a constant war that takes place in every situation e.g. we may be in a situation where we have worked hard and our pride wants everyone to know about it, so we boast about our deeds and how well we've done. God on the other hand doesn't work this way. His ways are of humility. He will show us this pride and how it influences our actions. Through the scriptures I was taught that we could deal with this old nature by confessing that it exists to God. He then in turn would cover it with his precious blood and transform it into His nature, thus helping us to grow and mature.

Every situation is a chance to know God in a new way. It's an opportunity to have our old nature cleansed. But constantly monitoring every little thing that you do is not easy as it can bring you into bondage. It can make you feel like you are a bad person because all you seem to deal with are the negative sides that dwell within you. As Christians we are always in the spotlight. Every detail of your life will be brought into question by friends, family and of course our own thoughts. We will constantly be told by all we encounter that Christians do not behave in that manner. Even our own inner thoughts will question our actions and make us feel that we are a bad witness for the Lord. It's up to us how we view all these negative responses. We can, if we choose, let them rule our lives and bring us into confusion. But we could end up putting up a false front for others to see e.g. when we are angry at someone, we will pretend that we are not and everything is fine. Our other choice is to be honest and confess the way we are feeling to God. We have to acknowledge that we have faults so God can exchange His nature for ours.

Confessing our faults to God and admitting to others that we are not perfect sounds so easy. What can be so hard about that, we may ask? The answer lies deep within our unconscious where Pharaoh (the ego) resides. He represents our proud nature that we inherited when Adam and Eve fell in the Garden of Eden. This proud nature rises up in everything that we do. It wants to always be in the spotlight. It wants everyone to think that we are a great person to know. It's this part of our nature that hates confessing to God or anyone else that we have done anything wrong.

This is how it works: First of all let's look at our proud will of revelation. Deep down within us our pride is telling us that we know best, our way is the only way and anyone who thinks differently is wrong. We then have our proud will of redemption that operates when our first line of defence has been proved to be wrong. If someone disagrees with what we have suggested, we will do whatever it takes to get our own way. We will lie, cheat or even use emotions to change someone else's opinion. These are just some of the ruses we use to redeem a situation. Finally our proud will of satisfaction comes into play. How smug we feel when we get our own way, when we can prove that someone else was wrong and we were right, when we can put them in the low place whilst we bask in the glory of our victory. No wonder it's very hard to genuinely admit to God that we are truly sorry for our actions. We may quite easily confess it outwardly, but to really mean it deep down and give it to God can prove to be very difficult indeed.

When I first became a Christian I have to admit there were times when humbling myself before God was the last thing on my mind. Sometimes the struggle between God and me went on for weeks but it always reached a peaceful ending. Through the years I've gradually come to recognise when my proud will is operating in a situation, when I am seeking to glorify myself instead of letting God's light shine through. It's much easier now to let God's revelation into a situation i.e. to ask what He wants out of these circumstances. Although there are still times when I try to work my problems out, I find it much easier to give them to God. I also find it more rewarding when God has worked a problem out. I don't feel smug or proud, I just thank the Lord for His goodness and the satisfaction I feel is in Him.

This book is based upon the scriptures that have led me in my walk with the Lord. I hope that these pages will inspire Christians and non-Christians alike to walk with God openly and honestly, and that they too may come to recognise the Lord as a friend. Many Christians struggle with their inner life, not understanding why they act like they do when the spirit of God dwells within them. Many Christians would rather pretend that they did not get angry or even that they have had perverse thoughts and feelings. They would rather pretend to be good, instead of confessing how they truly feel. When we look at the history of the Church and see how many ministers have been involved in all types of perverse actions, how much damage has been achieved because people are being led by inner desires that are only trying to glorify and satisfy their own selfish needs, it's clear to see that people are not aware of this deception that lies within.

I do believe that if Christians really faced up to the truth and confessed how they really felt, whether they were jealous or angry etc. and they gave these feelings to God and asked Him for forgiveness for feeling this way, then the Church would be stronger because it would be based upon God's truth, instead of man's deceit. Just by knowing that we have an ego that is operating within us that is causing us to act in ways that are not Christ-like can set so many people free from the bondage that they have been living in. It will explain to them why they have been doing things all their life without any victory.

I was one of those people who used to pretend that nothing affected me. I pretended that I didn't have emotions that I couldn't control. I tried to act as if I was perfect. I didn't feel that my actions were wrong because deep down I really did want to please the Lord, but I felt that if He saw me being angry etc. that somehow He would reject me. Having grown in the Lord I no longer feel this need to pretend. I have grown to the place where I can be honest with Him, confessing my faults gladly and knowing that He only reveals my old nature because He loves me. He knows what is within me, but He wants me to change so that I can become more like Him. When this process of dealing with the old nature becomes a part of our life it sets us free to be more honest with God. Firstly because we realise that God knows that our inner nature is there. Secondly because we know it is God who has revealed it to us and thirdly we know that we can confess this old nature to the Lord so that he can exchange it for His nature. No longer do we have to lie to God, others and ourselves about how we reacted in a certain situation or how we felt when someone had upset us. The burden is lifted. The devil cannot flog us anymore. We are free to be our true selves with God.

Chapter 2: God's call is to everyone

John 15v16: 'You have not chosen me, but I have chosen you.' We only have to look at our solar system to appreciate how special our planet Earth is. As we whirl through space we are governed by principles that were set up at the dawn of time. They guide us majestically in orbit around the sun; it all seems so effortless. As each one of us wakes every morning we take it for granted that these principles will still be working as the day before. The sun will shine, the clouds will blow past, and the rain will come at some point through the day. Then, as the day passes and we begin to look at the night sky, each star seems to be in place and the moon still reflects the light of the sun. We gaze in wonder, never really understanding the complexity of each planet and each star as they interact with one another. As far as we are concerned it's just another day, but to the scientists each day is a marvel. As technology improves, so does their understanding of it all. Their grasp of the interplay between the planets, stars and the cosmos is far greater than they ever could have imagined.

Earth is no less complex. It's constantly evolving around us and each day brings new surprises. One moment we are bathing in glorious sunshine, the next we are dealing with floods and storms. Our climate is so unpredictable we never know what is going to happen next. This can also be said about science. As it investigates the natural world around us we just never know what is around the corner waiting to be discovered. As technology and research advance every stone is being turned so that our understanding of the surrounding world is explored to its maximum. But it's not just today's world that we want to understand. Archaeology is using science and modern technology as never before to reveal secrets of the past. If they can understand the complexities of the past then maybe they can use all the information that they have gleaned to predict the future.

Having read all the above it seems like our thought of 'it's just another day' is more complex than we ever imagined. We also have to face the complexities of our own personal lives. Like the scientists that were mentioned earlier, who only understand the universe as they see it, we only understand the person we see in the mirror. The biggest part of us is hidden away from view in our unconscious. The real us only come out when we are placed under pressure, when we are angry, when we feel joy or passion and when we are scared. From a very young age we have built a personality around the real us. This personality fits into our surrounding world. We don't want to be the odd one out so we set in place many faces to fit many different situations. In every situation that we are faced with, our unconscious is working overtime to smooth our passage through that perceived crisis. It's at these times, if someone disagrees with our belief, that the anger and rage appear, or we feel sorry for ourselves because we were trying our best. We, like the universe, are far more complex than we could ever imagine.

To make things even worse we then have to fit into a society where everyone else is as complicated as we are. Each person has beliefs different to ours. What is important to them isn't important to us and vice versa. It may be that you are reading this book because you think it might give you an insight into what you believe is missing in your life. You may be a person that loves nature or you like to help people. Basically there is within your character a side of you that wants to benefit society and this world in some way. On the flip side to this your colleague or the person who you walk past on the high street has a totally opposite view point of life. They are not interested in books. No book can tell them what's missing in their lives; they believe that they have it all. They don't care about society. They don't care if the rainforests are being cut down. The only person they care about is themselves. The news is full of disturbing incidents that we would never be involved in; riots, rape, shootings, stabbings and murder. These atrocities are carried out by people who seem to be so very different from you. They have gone down a path that you would never walk. These disturbing scenes that we constantly see in the media can often deflate our aspirations to 'make the world a better place'. We look at the news and wonder if all our hard work that we do to improve our society is worth it.

To understand the complexities of life that we know, whether it's the world, society, our relationship with others or more importantly within ourselves, it's important that we understand why we are here. For some people life is just about living from day to day.

They earn money to pay the bills; any surplus goes on entertainment. But it's a routine that has no end; it just goes on and on. Every morning the alarm clock goes off; it's time for work. Each day brings a groan as they realise that they have to leave their warm bed and trudge off to do a job that they possibly hate. As they drive off, their minds are on other topics. They worry about the postman bringing bills that they can't pay, or their football team may have lost the night before. They pop into the garage for petrol or sandwiches and they encounter abuse from someone whose day is worse than theirs. All these experiences seem to make life so mundane. How can there be something else, when we have to face up to the prospect of encountering the same routines and the same people every day?

People have been having these same thoughts throughout history. Why are we here? What is the purpose of our lives? Why does the world have so many mysteries? Why does evil seem to be the dominating power that rules the world? There seems to be so many questions, with seemingly so few answers. If we want to understand the complexities of life then we have to understand the purpose of it. This is why people search throughout their whole lives, trying to find an answer to these questions, trying to find a purpose to their lives.

We have scientists telling us that we come from the universe. We have been involved in a wonderful journey, and when we die we go back to being a part of the universe once more. To me there is nothing wonderful about never existing again. I want an answer that involves *me* in the future. I don't want to think that when I die this is the end of everything for me. Many look to the stars for answers in another way. They are convinced that there are aliens who visit our planet. If they can find alien life then somehow they will find the answer to where man came from. Others seek answers through ghost hunting, psychic readings or spiritualism. They seek to find out if there is life after death, and they want to know what is on the other side. I am not going to go into it here, but it's important that people understand that although they may have felt comforted by these encounters, especially when they have supposedly spoken to a deceased loved one, they are not being helped spiritually. These days everyone seems to be into spiritualism and readings but if you mention Christianity they shun the very thought. The reason why people like spiritualism, tarot and other such things is because they don't have to make a commitment to anyone or anything. Whereas to be a Christian means that you have to commit to giving yourself to a higher power. Some people don't want to give up their self-rule and they settle for dealing with lower realms that don't give them any real answers to life. In fact, they only mask the truth and give people a false sense of security.

The Bible tells us we shouldn't talk to the spirits. Those who practice these arts say it's because the Bible is narrow-minded. The reason God doesn't want us to get involved with these powers is because He knows who these powers are controlled by and that they can't reveal the truth about the invisible spiritual world. They will only lead us onto the wrong path. It's a path that God does not walk.

We all have a desire to know more about life and its true meaning. We all go about trying to find out the answers in our own way. Each one of us is led to walk a different path, but it would be helpful if we knew where the path was and where it was leading us. In today's world we are faced with many topics that could keep us occupied throughout our lifetime. Each one gives a different insight into why we are on this planet. There are many religions and each one is slightly or totally different from the next. We are encouraged to follow their way if we want our lives to be perfect. There are also numerous mysteries scattered around, not just in England but throughout the world, that need investigating. They may or may not shed light on why we are here. With all these decisions to be made as to which way we travel, it would be a shame if at the end of our lives after all our hard work we found out that we had been looking in the wrong direction.

With this book I am trying to give you the spiritual equivalent of a Sat Nav that can lead you in the right direction. Once you have arrived it is then up to you to work out the small details through prayer and study. It may seem that the average person has their spiritual Sat Nav switched off. They couldn't care less about searching for the truth of their existence. They are happy in their nice homes, they are content with their jobs and the only thing that they want to focus on is where they are going on holiday. On the outside all seems well, but we only have to look at our own experience to know that on the inside they may be crying out for change and hate the way that they live. They are so unhappy; they want something real in their lives.

Through the scriptures of the Bible this book will try to show you that life without God is empty and a sham. I hope to show you that God is real and He wants to be a part of your life. He has a purpose for you and He will, if you let Him, be involved in every aspect of your life. No longer will you have to put up with those boring daily routines. Each new day will be a day where God walks alongside you. You will no longer have that empty feeling inside you, thinking that you are alone in this world. Instead, you will be filled with a joy that can't be fully explained in words.

I understand that you might be sceptical about these words, and you may be trying to work out what the catch might be. You could even be thinking that your life is perfect at this moment in time and it couldn't get any better. While you're pondering over all these thoughts, let me just say to you that whatever you have in your life, however good it seems, however fulfilled you think that you are, you are missing out on something that is far greater than you can ever imagine. God is far greater than the riches of this earth, which are very fleeting. The one thing we can be sure of when God is in our life is that he is always with us, not just in this life but also throughout eternity.

I can assure you that there is no catch. The only requirement of becoming a Christian is that we confess that we are sinners. We then have to confess these sins to God. We have to accept that Jesus Christ is our saviour and He paid the price for our sins when He died upon the cross. For this to happen, we have to realise that there is more to our universe than meets the eye. We may have to conclude that creation did not just happen by chance. If we decide that this is true, we then have to wonder about our own personal lives and the role we are playing on this planet. Have we been placed here just to make up the numbers? Or does the creator have a special purpose for us? If so, why are we separated from His presence? And why doesn't He reveal Himself to mankind?

The answers to the above questions are very simple. Firstly, we haven't just been placed upon earth to make the numbers up. Each individual is special to God and everyone will have a special place in His presence. Secondly, as we walk with Him we will come to realise that He has a purpose for each one of us i.e. for us to be as one with Him. I will answer the third and fourth questions together. God reveals Himself to man every day e.g. through man's natural surroundings we only have to observe creation to know that it didn't just happen by chance. We are just the right distance from the sun. Any nearer and we would burn up, if we were further away we would freeze. The angle of the earth is just right. There are numerous observations that I could write about creation and God's involvement but my book would be very long if I wrote every detail down. God is behind all of creation. His mark is everywhere, but the reason that we can't be in His presence on this planet is because we all have a sinful nature.

This sinful nature is within every person when they are brought into this world. It's a nature that only wants to live for self. The reason we are born with this nature is because in the Garden of Eden Adam decided that he didn't want to walk according to God's ways. He believed the serpent's lies that were full of deceit. This deceitful nature entered into man and as a result we were removed from God's presence. We were placed upon a lower realm, not with God's glory but with a deceitful nature. This nature has been passed down from generation to generation so that no one can escape its influence. It's this fallen nature that separates us from God.

No one likes to be called a sinner. It seems to convey the idea that we are an evil person, when we know that we are not. We may not be perfect, but we feel that our heart is in the right place and we do good when we can. To be called a sinner is an insult to our character and we resent this term being used. It's not a name that we want to be associated with and this causes us to stay away from the Church and ultimately from God.

Each person's fallen nature believes we are as God. It can't comprehend that we are sinful, which is why we have such difficulty confessing it. Our failure to confess this nature to God is the most important barrier that we have to overcome. In Hebrew the word 'sin' means to miss the mark. This mark is the standard that God sets for us to come into His presence. We have to remember who and what God is. He is pure and perfect. Any impurities that we may have would all be shown up the moment we tried to be one with Him. This is why we are called sinners. God is simply telling us that we are tainted and we don't reach His standard. If we want to be where He is then we have to humble ourselves and confess these imperfections to Him.

There is only one person who can make the decision to accept Jesus into your life i.e. you. Your friends may think you have gone mad. You may even lose their friendship altogether. It will take a great leap of faith on your part. God has given us all free will. He doesn't want robots who blindly love Him because it's the thing to do. He wants us to make up our own minds. He wants us to weigh up all the options and then make the decision to accept or to ignore what He is offering.

I would like to explain what becoming a Christian meant to me. As a sportsperson I didn't reach the great heights that I dreamt of but I did play at a fairly good standard. Through my career in football and cricket I won many trophies. It's a great feeling when everyone is applauding as you walk up to receive your reward for all the effort you have put in throughout the season. If you have ever won anything you will know what it feels like. I liken my experience of Christianity to winning a trophy. I would like you to think back when you last won something. Think of that exciting feeling that you got. It was a nice warm glow that lasted for hours, but it gradually faded away. Winning trophies doesn't even come close to the feelings that I have experienced in Christ. Multiply these feelings by a thousand and there is also the bonus that these feelings will always be with me. He doesn't fade out of my life. He is constantly with me. Each day brings a new desire to know Him more. I am not saying that you won't have hard times in your life when you may feel that He has left you. There will be some tough times ahead. But let me reassure you He will never leave or forsake you, and it is with this assurance that you can ask Christ into your life.

Accepting Christ into your life will be the best thing that you will ever experience. But the story doesn't end there. God's desire is for us to grow. He wants us to mature spiritually. We begin our spiritual lives like babies. We don't really understand the Word. His principles are often hidden from us, but as we walk with Him our knowledge will increase. As Christians we may be saved from sin but we are still controlled, especially as we take our first steps away from our old way of life. We want to be like Christ but we find that we are still behaving as before, which can be very frustrating. To become spiritual adults God has to remove this old nature and replace it with His own. His light shines into the dark recesses of our unconscious world and He exposes areas that are not pleasing to Him. He wants us to see these areas because He wants us to deepen our relationship with Him. It says in the Gospel of John if we confess our sins then we can walk in the light. His light is truth. The more we can exchange our darkness for His light and truth, the greater our experience with Him. Through the scriptures I hope to show you how you can change your old nature daily, which will allow you to be more like God. He is an all-consuming God which means that our sinful natures can't reside where he is, so to enter deeper into this truth we must change our ways. The more we change the more God can reveal His truth to us.

For those who don't give their lives over to Christ the Word of God will simply appear to be a book of stories; the Word will remain meaningless. It's only after we have given our lives to God that the Holy Spirit can move over the Word and bring it to life. It then becomes the most precious jewel that we own and we can't wait to read and study it because we know that God has something new and fantastic for us. One glorious little truth, when you know it's from God, can send shivers down your spine. It's so fantastic that it's hard to put into words. Accepting Jesus into our lives sets us on the road to a wonderful journey. He gives us an understanding of the complex world in which we live. He helps us to understand why we behave like we do. He gives us a purpose in a world that has lost its way. Do you want to remain in the darkness, or do you want to soar above in the wonderful light of God?

Chapter 3: Escaping Egypt

Walking with God through life's journey is the greatest pleasure man could ever have. It humbles me knowing that God created everything and wants to share my journey with me. But sadly some people's spiritual journey ends before it really gets started. They ask God into their lives, but then they sit back thinking all the hard work is done and carry on living as before. They don't invest time to discover what the Word of God actually means or spend time in prayer asking for God's guidance. For those that are humbled, their journey is a new adventure every day. The Bible is a source of great comfort. As they read and pray over the scriptures many secrets that were once hidden appear, shedding new light on everything.

In a letter to Timothy it tells us that all scripture is written down for our benefit, just like the instructions that come with a new appliance. If we don't read the manual then we might never find the channel that we want to watch on our new TV. As Christians we have two choices. By all means keep your Bible locked away in your drawer, hidden away from view. If this is what your spiritual life consists of, by all means behave this way. It won't stop God from being in your life, but what it will mean is that you will remain in darkness over what God is wanting from you, and what you can receive from Him. The second choice involves growing and maturing in God. It means spending time with the Word and in prayer. It's about getting to know God intimately so that He can direct us along the path to enlightenment.

The story in Exodus begins in Egypt, which can represent the world that we live in or it can mirror our own personal life. The Israelites were in bondage to a pharaoh. They were his slaves. Whatever he wanted them to build they had no choice in the matter, they had to obey. This reflects our lives in this modern world. We might think that we are free to do what we want, but in actual fact we are in bondage to the world's system of greed and living for self. If we want to understand this message on a personal level we can see this pharaoh as the little god who rules in our unconscious. We might think that we can live our lives just as we want, but what about the fears that rule our lives? E.g. we often don't achieve our goals because we are afraid of what others might think of us. What about the pride that makes us fall out with our best friends, just because we thought that we were right and they were wrong? Or the emotions that appear out of the blue that we have no control over? God comes into both these worlds and, if we will let Him, He can set us free. Not to just live how we want but to live, but to experience a freedom that only walking with God can bring.

We may not be able to change the world but we can change our own personal path. If we allow God into our lives, He can set us free from how others live. We will no longer have to walk in the footsteps of the Egyptians who worshipped false gods. The true God will help us to walk where He wants us to go. If you have lost your way, if you have forgotten your history i.e. that we were created by God to know Him, if you have become like the Israelites then God wants you to know that He has been listening all the time to your inner desires. He is calling you to follow Him wherever He may lead you.

It says in Exodus that Moses was told to tell the Children of Israel that God heard their prayers. God walks among us in many disguises listening to our prayers, but not just listening. He also answers each and every one. The answer might not be what we wanted or expected though. He gives us opportunities to grow spiritually. He opens up a way for us to leave the life of bondage and to discover Him. On this journey, as we are led forward spiritually, God will reveal to us how the lie that we inherited in the Garden of Eden has grown to dominate our lives. He will show us how and why the little god within us, represented by Pharaoh, has such a hold on our lives. He will show us why, when God is trying to lead us forward, we still experience the pull of Egypt that wants us to return to the former life that we thought we had left behind. To follow God means that we will have to face up to many truths that we won't like. God will also show us how much our old ways are ingrained within our unconscious and how it still affects our every decision even though we are Christians. As we shed our inner desire to live for self it will ultimately lead to God, fulfilling His promise to lead us to the Promised Land.

In Exodus 1v6-7 it says, 'they began to multiply and be fruitful and they began to increase in the land'. There are two ways that we can flourish in a land. We can either join ourselves to the country's system or we can flourish spiritually. In this case they had joined themselves to the ways of Egypt. They forgot that their roots were formed in the higher world that belongs to God and they had taken their eyes off spiritual matters. Pharaoh had complete control over them. They were there to do his bidding which was to build cities in his honour.

As Christians our whole lives should be dedicated to serving God. But there are times in our life, especially if we don't realise that God has called us to leave Egypt, when we are slaves to the world's system of living for self. We may have good intentions when planning the next day. We may think to ourselves that we will pray and read a passage from the Bible. But when the alarm clock goes off we forget that we had good intentions and we only remember the chores that need completing throughout that day. When the day is over and we switch the TV off, we sink into bed exhausted from all our hard work and we look forward to a good night's sleep. What doesn't cross our minds is that we have wasted another day spiritually. We have been so involved with building treasure cities for self that we have missed an opportunity to know God in a special way. This is what it means to be in bondage to the world's system. We have time to do all our chores and pastimes, but we never have time for God.

The book of Exodus is trying to show us that even if our lives seem to be flourishing, and it may seem that we have got treasure in abundance, our lives without God are still in bondage. We will always be afflicted by the world's system of greed. We will always have to pay taxes, experience illness, do jobs that we don't want to do. We grow old and die. When this happens all the monuments that we have built to glorify our name will one day be pulled down. So from that point of view, we will never escape the limitations that this world has to offer.

From the first verses in Exodus it's important to see that the real us is buried deep within our unconscious. It's hidden under all the false glamour that this world offers us. God comes along and tries to show us the truth. He gives us glimpses of Himself. His truth sinks to the very depth of the real us and it begins to ask questions. It wants answers and it causes confusion because it goes against everything that we have ever believed. It's this new nature that causes all the conflict within as we struggle to set ourselves free from the old nature that is the dominant force at present. This battle between the two natures is a fight to the death because the ego doesn't want to be set free. It's happy ruling, and we will see later how Pharaoh hardened his heart when Moses asked him to set God's people free. This hardening of the heart is because Pharaoh thinks his reign is coming to an end and he doesn't like it. If you are truly seeking God you may not realise that this battle between the real you that God created and your ego is going on. As we become aware of this conflict within, it's easier to see how circumstances in the past have been dominated by our old nature.

The Children of Israel had lost their way and in v8 it says, 'There rose up a new King over Egypt, which knew not Joseph'. Joseph reflects the mature Christian who has experienced much tribulation in his life, yet he has still managed to put his trust in God. Joseph was made second-in-command in the land of Egypt. Only Pharaoh was above him. He had mastered the world that he lived in. He had so dominated his worldly desires that not even Pharaoh could lead him astray. He put God first in every decision that he made. As a result of his actions he was allowed to roam free throughout all of Egypt being a witness to God and bringing sustenance to the people. If it wasn't for Joseph the land would have perished. Although this story shows how a young boy became master over Egypt, it also reveals to us an inner journey that we have to face to become ruler over our own life. This is a spiritual state into which we can grow. But, like Joseph, we have to be willing to put God first, which is not an easy thing to do. Joseph was tested in many areas throughout his life to see where his loyalties were. He was hated by his brothers, he was thrown into prison for something he didn't do and he went through many trials, yet still he trusted God every step of the way. His faith in God gave him victory. Although it took many years, he was finally allowed to rule over Egypt.

It's absurd to think that any Christian can forget that God should be at the very centre of all they do, but sadly for many this seems to be the case. They forget their calling and they live their lives pretty much like everyone else. They allow their inner Pharaoh to take control. He knows nothing of Joseph or anything spiritual. His only concern is to make sure that the self is satisfied. He rules with an iron fist, quickly stamping on any opposition to him. In this state, the spiritual side to our nature is completely dominated. With no vision of God, it bows before the ego accepting its rule.

In v.10 it says 'come, let us deal wisely with them; lest they multiply'. This reminds me of when Adam and Eve fell in the Garden of Eden, when the serpent tricked Eve into desiring the fruit from the tree because it would make her wise. This inner deceit runs through each of us and it tricks us into believing that it knows best. It tricks us into believing that building treasure cities for self is the best way to live our lives. The last thing that Pharaoh desires is to see the Children of Israel (our spiritual side) multiplying. He knows that if they multiply then they could take over Egypt (our lives) and he (ego) will lose his position as ruler over their lives.

Our egos will go to great lengths to trick and side-track us from our original purpose in life. If we look at how the unconscious works on a natural level we will see this deceit. We have decided that we need to lose a few pounds so we go on a diet. One day, although we have been very strict with ourselves, a cream cake is presented before us. Our inner nature that wants this cake will find plausible excuses as to why we can have that cake now. It will also make the promise that we will work off the pounds that we might gain...tomorrow. We eventually give in and eat the cake but of course tomorrow we forget our deal. The ego knows which buttons to press to get its own way. We may think that we are in control but the truth is we are not. Remember your ego has plenty of years of experience dealing with your inner nature.

In the Exodus story Pharaoh side-tracks them into building treasure cities for him. He doesn't want to fight them because in v9 he has already recognised that the Children of Israel are mightier, so the only way he can win this battle is to get them involved in another grand project. He wants them to feel that they are achieving their goal. Any time that we show signs of spiritual growth the Pharaoh within us begins to panic. If he's not careful he is at risk of losing everything, so he begins to press those buttons that I have just mentioned. He devises a plan to keep the spiritual side subdued and he forced the Israelites to gradually come under the physically binding regime of the worldly life. For his plan to work the Israelites had to be driven into carrying out these tasks, so in v11 it says that Pharaoh got 'taskmasters to afflict them with their burdens'. We have always got a task to do, whether it's working, gardening, practicing football etc. in fact anything that stops us from getting closer to God. These tasks bring along their burdens with them. We think that if they are not achieved then we can't do spiritual things because these have to be done first. The ego will always afflict us with these types of burdens and we fall for them every time e.g. we haven't planted flowers in the garden for 12 years, but all of a sudden if we don't do it right now, it will be a disaster. Friends will turn up out of the blue whom you haven't seen for 6 months and they want you to go out with them. The next day something else will be in the way and before you know it the new joy that you were beginning to feel getting closer to God has disappeared.

The next part of the verse says 'and they built for Pharaoh treasure cities, Pithom and Raamses'. The ego has got us building monuments to make us look important in this world. We are building them for self-worth. If we have homes or trophies that people can admire it makes us feel important and valued. We spend our lives building our dream homes, having the best cars, we will only eat at the swankiest restaurants and it is all to make people think that we are important. When looking back at history we can see that all the pharaohs built many monuments to show how grand they were. They tried to leave a legacy on this earth showing all the great things that they had achieved, and this is what our ego is trying to do.

In v12, it says 'the more they afflicted them, the more they grew'. Pharaoh made the lives of the Israelites very tough. Without the Lord, the ego creates a life of bondage. He can make it seem as if we are flourishing, but the truth is we are not. We are only building earthly things that won't last. I have seen this happen many times in others. They are so caught up in their own little world. They think that they are building for a great future. They flog themselves to death trying to achieve their dream of having a nice house. They work many hours and before they know it life has passed them by.

They are left with bricks and mortar and then they die.

I love to watch *Time Team* on TV when archaeologists dig up the past. They dig a field in the middle of nowhere. They then come to the conclusion that a palace used to be here. Even the bricks and mortar have gone, not just the people who built the palace and the people who lived there. They no longer exist, their lives are over and no one can remember how grand that house was. They can only imagine. With God we have a heavenly home that will last forever. It will be there throughout eternity and all we have to do is accept Christ into our lives as Saviour.

We can see in v15-22 that the next stage of Pharaoh's plan is to kill all the male children that are born. Even though this is happening to the Israelites there is always the chance that they could return to the Lord, so in the following verses we can see the next part of his plan is to attain complete mastery of his own world and kill off the spiritual side once and for all. Pharaoh tells the midwives to kill the male children and to save the females. This way there would be no redeemer which would mean that they would have to stay in Egypt and bondage forever.

The midwives names were Shiphral and Puah which in Hebrew mean brightness and splendid. They represent something within us that is opposed to what Pharaoh or the ego wants. In v17 it says 'they feared God'. There is buried deep within us all a bright light that desires to find God. We may not know that it's God who we are looking for, we may be just searching for something that satisfies us, something that our egos can't give us. Deep within our unconscious we are asking questions about our world, our life, where we came from, what the future is going to bring. To everyone else these questions are hidden away but God sees and He answers our questions, but sometimes it takes a long time for the answers to come to our notice.

There is an important lesson to be learned here i.e. God's ways are not our ways, neither are His thoughts like our thoughts. We live in a modern society that expects every situation to be resolved immediately e.g. if our boiler breaks down, we expect the plumber to stop what job he is doing and come and fix it immediately. We don't care that someone else might be cold. In our eyes we are more important than they are, so we should be top priority. We can be like this as Christians. When a problem enters our life we assume that God will fix it straight away. When our prayers are not answered immediately we blame God and say 'He is not fair', 'He doesn't love us after all', and 'Why do we bother praying?' Little do we realise that God is working behind the scenes waiting for the exact time when His help will be most beneficial.

Moses was their redeemer but before he was mature enough to set them free he had to experience Egypt for himself and then he had to make the choice using free will to leave and find God. There are many people who ask God for help that have a burning desire to be free from the way that they live. Like Moses they don't want to live in a world that's full of grandeur and selfishness so they ask God to reveal Himself and find a way out. But sadly for these people, because God doesn't answer their questions or prayers immediately or He doesn't reveal Himself in a way that they thought He should, they seek satisfaction elsewhere. They turn to drink, drugs or they bury their desires into something carnal, believing God doesn't exist or He is ignoring them.

Following on with the story we see that Pharaoh does not give up. He still wants all the male children killed. This must have been distressing for the parents of Moses. Their newborn baby was going to be killed unless something drastic happened. How could they protect their son? It must have been a dreadful situation to be in. Placing him in a basket amongst the bulrushes may seem strange to us but they were putting their trust in God.

Pharaoh knows that if the male seeds grow then the Israelites will become stronger and his reign will come to an end. He has a plan to stop this from happening but he hasn't reckoned on God's intervention. When we commit the small life that is beginning to grow within our unconscious to God, then He will use all His power to keep us safe. When we are faced with these circumstances it's always good to remember the scripture Romans 8v28. It tells us that all things work together for good, to those who love God. It doesn't just say the good things; it also includes the bad times that we experience. We can see this principle in action with the life of Moses. If we put our faith in God even the situations that threaten to kill us off spiritually can work in our favour. They bring us to the place where God wants us to be. In Moses' case he was brought into Pharaoh's court.

If we look in the book of Genesis and the full story of Joseph we can see this principle in action. In Genesis 50v20 Joseph's brothers thought that he was going to get revenge on them, when Jacob their father died, for what they had done to him. They had treated Joseph badly, casting him into a pit then selling him into slavery. But when they stood before him fearing the worst, he comforted them with the words 'you thought you were doing evil to me when you carried out all these actions, but God was behind the scenes working out everything for good. He was using all things to bring us to this place that we are now in'. It's important to remember this principle because God will use both good and bad situations that we experience for our good. Even though Pharaoh seems to be in control and he is doing wicked things in the lives of the Children of Israel, God is using all these atrocities to bring them to a place where they will eventually be set free.

The parents of Moses were Amram, which means

'kindred of the high' and his wife was called Jochebed and her name means 'divine splendour'. Amram was known as an upright man and his wife was also known for her spiritual quality, being the daughter of Levi. We can see from their names that God was an important part of their lives. Because of this special union that they had they put their trust in God over what happened to Moses. Sadly many people, unlike Amram and Jochebed, go through life trusting in their own strength. They think that they are strong enough to fight off and deal with all that life sends to test us. They end up having breakdowns, being stressed out or taking pills from the doctor, because the truth is we cannot deal with the pain of life. God doesn't want us to take on the might of Egypt and Pharaoh alone. He wants us to put our trust in Him and He will fight our battles for us.

This is why Jesus says in Matthew 11v28-30 'come unto me, all ye that labour and are heavy-laden, and I will give you rest'. Jesus is saying 'give me all your problems. You are not strong enough to carry your burdens. All these things are happening to show you how much you need me'. Another important point to bring up here is the fact that as believers of God, Moses' parents also knew that if it wasn't God's will that Moses should live and be taken from them they knew that it was not the end of him. His spirit would return to God. They knew that one day they would all be together again in the afterlife.

In order to protect Moses from being killed, v3 tells us that Jochebed 'built him an ark of bulrushes and daubed it with slime and with pitch and put the child therein'. We can read this story and take it as face value and accept the writer's account that this is what actually happened or we can look at it through spiritual eyes and try to understand its deeper meaning. As Christians this story reveals the principles that will keep us safe when faced with a situation over which we have no control. It shows us that although we may be in darkness, placed on a river (path) that could lead us anywhere we are actually in God's safe hands. We are being watched over by the Holy Spirit, making sure that we end up in the exact place where God wants us to be.

Not only does Moses survive when he is rescued from the river, he is then given back to his mother so she can nurse him and raise him. We may think if Moses had died he could not have given him back. This is true, but when these times come upon us God will strengthen us and bless us in many other different ways. Death does occur. It is not God punishing us or that he wants to see us feeling sad. It's a natural process that occurs because of the fall in the Garden of Eden. We also have to remember that to God death is not the end. That loved one is in God's presence and he knows that you will see that person again. If you don't know God as our saviour or you don't believe that there is an afterlife, death to you is the ultimate end. The loss of a loved one can have a devastating effect on your life. What can anyone say to comfort you? But for me, and thousands of others, death is only a brief interlude, a brief separation until we all meet again with God and our departed loved ones.

Moses' story reflects the new life that we can have with God. When he is pulled out of the water he is raised and educated in Egypt. His education is symbolic of our awakening consciousness as it learns all it needs to operate in this realm. His education helped him to move around Egypt quite easily and to take part in everything that Egypt had to offer. This is part of life's journey. We experience every aspect of what this world has to give us. We indulge ourselves in every fad that is relevant at the time, expecting it always to be the most fulfilling experience ever. But if we are honest, it never is. We then move on to the next craze and so on and so on but life never seems to fulfil its promise, we are always left wanting more.

In Exodus 2 v11-12, it says 'when Moses was grown he went out unto his brethren and looked on their burdens: and he spied an Egyptian smiting a Hebrew'. Moses was the prince of Egypt but there came a time in his life as it will in ours when we see that the so-called joys of this world are oppressing us and stopping us from being one with God. Moses had grown. He was aware of all the joys that Egypt could offer him, yet he went to his brethren and saw the truth of what was occurring and it was then that he killed an Egyptian. Moses represents the spiritual side of us that wants something more. His eyes were opened to the truth. It might seem that building treasure cities for self is a great idea, but it comes at a cost. Moses sees that there is more to life than serving Pharaoh (our selfish needs).

He knows that if he is to be set free then he has to do something about the situation, so he killed the Egyptian. For the first time the oppressive side of his nature has no hold over him, so it's with a clear head that he makes the decision to leave.

This struggle between the side of us that is created by God and the ego/Pharaoh is happening every day throughout the world. God wants the enslaved spiritual side of us to see the truth about this world. He will do everything within His power to show us that this life is a sham, but the choice to be set free has got to come from within us. God may show us, when we go to church or when we talk to our friends or through reading this book, if we are sincerely seeking to know more about Him then He will show us what is stopping us from knowing Him in a greater way. He will reveal to us the areas of our nature that are keeping us oppressed. He will show us that the pleasures of this world are not all that they seem to be.

Moses saw the worldly Egyptian side of us dominating the enslaved side of us that should have been worshipping God. To know more of God we have to make a choice. In Moses' case he killed the Egyptian thus setting him on the road to freedom. In our case we have to accept that we are sinners and ask Jesus into our lives. We then have to be willing to forsake all and learn of Him instead. Moses no longer desired the glory of this world that Egypt offered. All the glamour had gone, but he was not strong enough to face Egypt head-on and tackle the problems that were being enforced on the Children of Israel. His next move was to flee into Midian where he probably thought that he could hide away, but God had other plans.

When the choice of following God is put before us, we will have to make one of the hardest decisions of our lives. First let's look at the people who refuse to accept that following God is better. What have they got to look forward to? They carry on following their dream and they continue to build treasure cities that do not last. Each day they grow older until finally the day comes when their life expires. The person who chose God will follow a different path. Yes, they too will also have dreams that they want to follow but now they are not based upon selfish motives. If they don't come to pass it's not the end of the world, God will have something better for us. We will also grow old and eventually die but the difference is we will have an eternity with God.

The choice we make to follow God is not an easy one because it will bring you on a collision course with some people. Friends may forsake you and some people may ridicule you and even despise you. Moses was brought up as Pharaoh's son but when he had made his decision he was despised by Pharaoh, so much so that he wanted to kill him. Following Christ and separating yourself from the ways of the world can be a lonely path to walk. This is because you know deep down that the normal daily routines that people have is not what you want anymore. Our new life alienates us in so many areas but to those that walk this path it's all worth it. Many people in the world are lonely even though they are surrounded by friends and possessions. The difference is we will always have Jesus with us.

Exodus 2v15: 'Moses fled from the face of Pharaoh, and dwelt in the land of Midian.' Escaping a situation to avoid it is not always a good idea because at the back of your mind the problem will still be there eating away at you. Moses may have originally left for this reason because he didn't want to face up to Pharaoh, but this wasn't God's reason for letting him leave. He had other plans for Moses, plans that even Moses could not have imagined.

We can as Christians use God as a way of escapism. We may have areas in our unconscious that need to be brought before God so that he can cleanse them, but instead of facing these facets of our nature we run away. If we are going to grow and mature in God then He will at some stage in our life bring us face to face with the problems that we left behind. He wants us to overcome these areas so that we can experience His forgiveness. Moses may have left Egypt but later on in his life he is asked to return to face up to Pharaoh and with God's help he is to break the shackles that once held him. The moment we realise that this world has nothing to offer is the time that we have to ponder what our next move is going to be. We know that God is calling us but we need time to work everything out. It's such a big decision, one that can't be rushed.

In v15 it says ''He sat down by a well'. Having removed himself from the influences of Egypt, it says that Moses came to a well because he probably knew that he wanted to drink from something deeper, something more fulfilling. The well is a symbol of truth and nourishment. This can be seen when Jesus spoke to the woman at the well when he visited Samaria. He told her the truth about her life. As we throw our bucket into the well, God will begin to reveal truths to us that we didn't realise. He will cast light on various situations that will help us to form an opinion, but He will never force you to follow that light. That choice has to be yours. The waters of the Word contain many secrets. Some are clear and easily understood but they also have depth. Others are hidden from view. It's up to us to find them through God's help as we pray and study.

Water in the Word often reflects our inner nature. It shows how we are reacting in our unconscious to the situation that we find ourselves in. Exodus 14v13 Moses says to the people 'be still and see the salvation of the Lord'. In this situation, which is also to do with water, Moses wants the people to still their unconscious thoughts so they can see God in action. Whilst we are running to and fro in our minds trying to work things out for ourselves, trying to redeem the situation through our proud will, we will never hear the voice of God. If we truly make the commitment to follow God, then He will not leave us floundering and He will give us guidance.

Exodus 2v21-22: Moses at this stage decides to stay in Midian. He realised that he couldn't return to Egypt because Pharaoh would have him killed, or at least imprisoned. In relation to our own spiritual walk, this period signifies a time in our lives when we are content with our decision to follow God but it's also a strange place to be in because we are not really sure what is expected from us. It says in v23 'the King of Egypt died'. His death releases more inner groaning from the Children of Israel. If we don't remember that Pharaoh, Moses and the Children all reflect the battle that is raging within us then all this might sound confusing. It's our continual crying out to the Lord in the midst of this battle that allows Him to return Moses. God knows the only way that we will ever be free spiritually is to separate ourselves from the influence of Egypt once and for all. Jesus' death for us upon the cross and our acceptance of Him as Saviour is the only way you can be freed from this world of sin.

Exodus 3v7-9: 'I have surely seen the affliction of my people who are in Egypt'. Moses was now in the right place. We may think that God just allows situations to drag along without really caring for us and how we are feeling, but this is not true. God listens to all our prayers and He answers every one but not always immediately. If God had allowed Moses to return to Egypt before he had grown spiritually, then he would not have had the strength to deal with Pharaoh. Our own inner growth can often dictate how and when God can move i.e. if we have not grown spiritually then God can't remove some situations from our life. In God's mercy he allows them to stay until the time that we can remove them completely from our lives.

In 3v10 God tells Moses 'Come now therefore, and I will send thee unto Pharaoh that thou mayest bring forth my people'. If we are going to follow God on an inward journey to the Promised Land, to a place where we have grown and matured into a spiritual adult, then we will have to decide at some point that Pharaoh (the ego) must be removed from power and we will have to install a new king to rule over us i.e. Jesus Christ. Even though Moses encounters God on Mount Horeb and hears Him speak from out of the midst of the burning bush, Moses knew that the battle with Pharaoh was not going to be an easy one. After all, Pharaoh has been in control a long time. He could destroy Moses and Aaron with one word to his guards. In our unconscious Pharaoh has this same power. He has manipulated every situation to suit his own end. If it wasn't for God working behind the scenes, he would take all of our ideas of being free from his rule and he would destroy them. Moses knows that he can't break Pharaoh's hold over his people alone, as we can see by his reply in the next verse. Moses asks God in v11, 'who am I?' He realises that he can't set them free, God has to be the one to do it. Yes, God will be the one to set them free, but we are the ones who have to show that we have made a free will choice to follow God's ways so ultimately it will be down to us to face up to Pharaoh and denounce his rule over us.

In Exodus 4 Moses sets off on his journey and when he reaches Egypt he meets up with his brother Aaron. Moses talks about what has been happening on a higher spiritual level, whereas Aaron talks about the worldly life of Egypt. They meet up with the spiritual elders of the Children of Israel, which represent the mature parts of self. It is the part of us that asks for the truth to be revealed. To convince the elders that they have come from God, Aaron speaks the Word of God whilst Moses shows the miraculous signs of God through the rod etc. The inner self acknowledges these signs and bows itself down in submission (v31), eagerly wondering what God is about to do to free them from Egypt. We are now ready to make the final commitment to God.

Exodus 3v19-20: God says, 'I am sure that the King of Egypt will not let you go, no, not by a mighty hand'. God goes on to say in the following verse that He is going to have to smite Egypt with all His wonders before Pharaoh finally gives in. Before Moses and Aaron go to see Pharaoh, God has already informed them that their words will fall on deaf ears. But when Pharaoh ignores their pleas they don't recall His words. The same can be seen in the New Testament when Jesus warned His disciples of what lay ahead for Him, but when the actual events were occurring they forgot his words. They panicked and thought that all their dreams had come to an end. It was much later after the events had taken place that they recalled His words.

When Moses and Aaron saw Pharaoh to proclaim God's message, their countenance according to Jewish tradition was so bright that it caused the Egyptian scribes to throw down their books and kneel before the higher power that was before them. When we are confronted with God's Word and Spirit part of us knows without a doubt that God reigns supreme. This side of our nature will always bow in reverence but God has given us all free will which is governed by our ego. It's this part of our nature that doesn't want to recognise God's Word.

Our modern world is based upon facts. As we have grown in knowledge, the need for God has steadily declined. Tangible truths are now the building blocks of our society. The credibility of the scientist far outweighs the outdated knowledge of the priest who only talks about a God that we never see. This principle can be seen in many areas, not just religion. If it's not been scientifically proven then it can't be true.

Knowledge and the inner belief that we are the gods of our own universe are obstacles that we have to overcome if we are to venture to the Promised Land.

Scientists may be able to explain how certain principles in the universe operate, but mainly their knowledge is limited. With every new theory that they come up with to shed new light on our surroundings and how we came into existence a new question arises shedding doubt on what we previously thought.

Exodus 5v7: 'Ye shall no more give the people straw to make brick, as heretofore: let them go and gather straw for themselves'. When straw is mentioned in the Word of God, it's a term that is used for satisfaction. The bricks they were making were being used to build Pharaoh's cities. Egypt would then be one of the greatest nations that the world had seen. If Egypt was prosperous then they would ultimately benefit from its riches. By increasing their workload they didn't have time to think about God and leaving Egypt. He wanted them to concentrate solely on gathering straw. In relation to our spiritual walk, the battle for freedom has begun between Pharaoh within (ego) and the spiritual side that wants to escape his rule. If we allow Pharaoh to have his way then anything new that we experience will die and be forgotten. Our concentration on gathering satisfying items around us will increase and our lives will become more intolerable as our bondage in this world increases.

When Moses came back to Egypt and told the Israelites what God was going to do, they must have been so excited. At last they were going to be free to do what they wanted. They might not have envisaged leaving Egypt for good but maybe they thought they would be in control of their own destiny. Yet here they are, working even harder to get the same job completed. Our natural response when our best plans are shattered is to have a good moan to our friends and family. We hope that they will show sympathy and that they will back up our point of view. But if we are going to be spiritual in our outlook then we have to change the way we view the situations that we find ourselves in. We should be like Moses who went to God and asked what was happening. He didn't blame the Israelites. He was honest with God and told him that he didn't understand. It was only after he humbled himself before God that God revealed what He was going to do. We should always seek God in prayer when something has happened that we don't understand. We should never blame Him because situations come along for a reason.

When we pray and seek God's guidance He will always answer. We might not be aware of it but He will be working behind the scenes making sure that His plans are fulfilled. At times, as we see in Exodus 5v15-23, it will seem that God has got it all completely wrong. It will seem that God is only interested in bringing evil upon us, but I can assure you that this is not the case. God has our best interest at heart, but sometimes He exposes the doubts and fears that lie within our unconscious so that we can confess them before Him. It's only when we have confessed our fears and doubts before Him that we can be cleansed inwardly and God can move onto the next phase of His plan.

Exodus 6v1: 'The Lord said unto Moses, now shalt thou see what I will do to Pharaoh: for with a strong hand shall he let them go, and with a strong hand shall he drive them out of his land.' If we are sincerely seeking God then He will always reveal His will to us. God's only true desire is for us to be free of Pharaoh's rule. He wants us to see that all the false gods that we worship in this land can't bring true happiness. He wants to drive out all these false beliefs that we have and replace them with belief in Him.

The story continues in Exodus 7v10 with Moses and Aaron obeying God. In the previous verses God once more informs Moses and Aaron what their involvement is going to be in their next encounter with Pharaoh. He also reiterates what Pharaoh's response is going to be. It seems their resolve is growing because, even though God informs them that Pharaoh's heart will be hardened and he will not listen to them, they still went along with God's plan and stood before Pharaoh.

This encounter with Pharaoh reveals how the deceitful nature within us can be overcome when we join our will with God's. When Moses and Aaron encounter Pharaoh on this occasion they threw a rod down upon the floor and it became a serpent. If someone did that in front of me I would run a mile, but we can see in v11-12 that this impressive feat didn't impress Pharaoh. He simply asked his magicians to do the same. In response to Moses casting down his rod the magicians did the same and their rods also turned into serpents.

Man's deceitful nature will always try to replicate what

God has done and will try to prove that if man can achieve this without God's help then there isn't a need for God. We may not be aware that we are doing this but when we try to understand the world around us by delving into areas that we shouldn't, if we do not involve God then we are using our deceitful nature. We are actually saying that we do not need God. We can achieve all that we require without His help. The warning here to all those who use sorcery or magicians to replicate what God achieves can be seen in v12 when Aaron's serpent/rod swallows up all the magician's serpents. We all have this deceitful nature within that seeks to be all-powerful but God is showing us that to grow and mature then this deceitful nature has to be removed.

The magicians were able to create an illusion and use it to distort the reality and understanding of anyone that was watching. We often use our deceitful will to try and create illusions that we want others to see. We do this to get our own way and trick others into believing that our ways are right when in actual fact they are full of deceit. Moses and Aaron were quite different because they were one with God. They had no deceitful motives which meant that they could work a miracle by *actually* making the rod change its form and giving it the ability to eat the other serpents. God's truth will always overcome the deceitful work of the devil who operates through people.

In Hebrew the word miracle means sign or wonder. When watching TV we can watch some truly fantastic illusions that will have us all wondering how it was achieved. This is what magic is all about. To some people magic and miracles can seem like the same thing. Both events are spellbinding but we have to realise that magic is through a person manipulating objects around him to gain glory for himself, whereas miracles are God changing the physical surroundings to show His glory.

Having seen what was revealed, the scriptures tell us that Pharaoh's heart was hardened. We can see a similar response by the scribes and Pharisees in the New Testament who, after seeing Jesus carry out numerous miracles, had their hearts hardened and their response was to get angry. Eventually, as their anger grew, their desire to have Jesus removed grew too, until finally they sent Jesus to His death on the cross. Many heard Jesus speak but never really listened and they turned their backs and ignored Him, whereas others who heard Him speak responded to His words and gave their lives to him. Even today when Christians share with others how Jesus has saved them and how He has worked miracles in their lives, there will still be the same mixed responses. Many will harden their hearts and call it rubbish, whereas others who are seeking God themselves will gladly rejoice with you and accept God's grace into their lives.

Exodus 7v14-25: After the battle of wills represented by the rod turning into a serpent, Moses is told by God to turn the waters of the River Nile into blood. When God strikes out at Pharaoh He begins by challenging the very life force that flows through Egypt. In our unconscious we want to be like Egypt. We want to be powerful in our own world. We want everyone to see that we are a force not to be messed with. In this modern world we mustn't show any signs of weakness. If we do then people will try to invade our space and conquer us. They will take advantage of us and we will have to submit to what they want.

The reason that we fear God entering our lives is because He challenges all of this. He will reveal to us that we are not powerful. We are not in charge; everything that we have is down to God. It's nothing to do with Pharaoh/ego sitting upon the throne in our unconscious. There have been many kings throughout history who have ruled vast empires, many great sporting heroes, businessmen who have amassed great wealth, great scientists who have understood many secrets of nature and space, but every single one has died and left everything they achieved behind. The Pharaoh within us thinks that he can live and rule forever. But God shows us that we are like a flower that for a short time basks in the glory of the sun, but then it withers and dies.

Let's look at how God challenges our rule: In v19 it states that there will be blood in the vessels of wood and stone, both being substances with which they made their false gods. The waters of the Nile represent everything that we think brings us life. Today's youth are into partying, drinking and taking drugs. It will vary from generation to generation, depending what the trend is at the time. The more mature person will be seeking stability in their home, how they can make their money last throughout their life time. They want their money to last so that they can spend it on meals, buying their next car, and also so they can take a nice vacation somewhere exotic.

When God turned the waters into blood He was showing how everything that we put our trust in can change so quickly. Too much drink or drugs and we can be in hospital fighting for our lives, stock markets can crash leaving us in terrible debt. We will no longer be able to afford our homes or plan any more holidays. The commodities that we worshipped no longer bring the life that we were expecting. Instead they now bring death to our inner lives.

It's not just property or our finances that can change quickly. Recently I have lost a few friends who have died of cancer. Our bodies are not made to last forever. We only have to hear the news every day to see how many people's lives have been devastated by murder, floods, earthquakes and cyclones. One of the biggest illusions that we encounter is the thought that it will never happen to us, or if it does then we can get it fixed. God is striking at the heart of everything that we hold dear and He is showing us that it's all temporary. It can be removed and taken from us in an instant. God is also showing, by replacing the water with blood, that true life can only come if we put our trust in Him.

Exodus 7v22: 'The magicians did so with their enchantments'. Pharaoh, faced with this disaster, turns to his magicians to see if they can replicate what Moses has done. The world will always try to achieve what God has done because deep down we think that we are far more important than we really are. We can't believe that the situation we are facing can bring death, so we look for a way out. If we can find an escape route i.e. through manipulating our surroundings, then we will have no need for God and we will harden our hearts once more. After the magicians had performed their magic Pharaoh's heart was hardened. He was convinced that God had done nothing special. Our unconscious only sees what it wants to see. This is why so many people fall for the tricks that fraudsters play.

A sudden change in our daily routine caused by God should bring about a reaction within our unconscious.

We will either be like Pharaoh who seeks to find answers from the science of the day, or we could, if we are already Christians, blame God for bringing this destruction into our lives. The final choice that we have is to accept that God is trying to reveal to us that the pleasures we seek in Egypt are only fleeting. They will fade away and unfortunately, if we have put our faith in them, one day we will be left with nothing.

Exodus 12v29-36: Many people joke about Christians seeing the light, but this is exactly what happens. God comes to us and He reveals the sinful nature that we inherited at the fall. He sheds light upon it and for the first time we actually see the world for what it is. When we first become a Christian, God enters our life and He offers His protection. He gives us the blood of Jesus to hide behind as He moves forth to destroy the firstborn sin that dwelt at the very core of our deceitful nature. Pharaoh, who represents our proud nature, stands down and he hands his authority over to God. He concedes that God is greater so we can leave Egypt and follow God. In v31 he even tells us to go and serve the Lord.

Now Pharaoh has lost his authority but this is not the last time that we will feel his presence as he still tries to influence our every decision. Pharaoh has lost his kingdom but he still fights on. He returns in many disguises belittling God's leadership in the hope that he can persuade us to return to Egypt. God will lead us into circumstances to reveal how much we are not like Him, how our nature is still full of deceit that needs cleansing. In these times God wants us to humble ourselves and confess our faults before Him. Pharaoh on the other hand will be using these situations to show us that we are worthy of more and God doesn't really love us. If He did then we wouldn't have to suffer. He gives us plausible reasons why we should return to Egypt. As the Children of Israel leave Egypt to follow God we will see them encounter some of the spiritual battles that we will face. The scriptures reveal that there will be some Israelites (Christians) who will want to return to Egypt, some will die in the wilderness, and a few will make the long arduous journey to Canaan where the marriage of their hearts to God will take place.

Revelation 21v2: 'And I John saw the holy city, New

Jerusalem, coming down from God out of Heaven, prepared as a bride adorned for her husband.' The bride is only interested in being prepared and adorned for her husband. She is only interested in pleasing him. She isn't interested in anyone else. For the marriage to be a great occasion the bride has got to commit herself to it. No one can make her do so; it's got to be her free will decision. To make ourselves ready we have to use the provision that God has given us i.e. the blood of Jesus. The Israelites sacrificed animals daily. They believed that the animals' blood would take away their sins. We can use the blood of Jesus on a daily basis to forgive us of our inner nature that is unlike God's.

Jesus is the Lamb of God because He was our sacrifice. He died in our place and shed His blood so that we can be forgiven. When the Lord returns He will be looking for someone who has changed their nature so much that they will be able to enter into his glorious presence. When we were created by God it was with the intention that we should be one with Him, that we should have a special union with Him. But all this fell apart in the Garden of Eden. God has never forgotten His desire to be one with us. He has constantly revealed

Himself throughout history showing us the way that we can return to Him and once again take part in a special union. If we remain in Egypt and live life as we did before we got saved, just using the name of Jesus as an afterthought to imply that we are kind and good, then we are really saying that although we believe in the Lord we don't want to make a commitment. We want to be in charge of our own lives and we can live very well without His intervention.

When we are born into this natural world we are born of the seed of our parents and that seed carries within it the seeds of all sin. Because we are born of a corruptible seed, straight away our physical body begins to die. The Bible talks about man being born again in 1 Peter 1v23. Not by the seed of man, but by the seed of God and this seed is incorruptible so there is no sinful nature involved. This seed can never sin, and it can never die. This is why the Bible says that when we are born again we have eternal life and this new nature can never know death because it's already passed from death into life. 1John 3v9 says, 'whosoever is born of God doth not commit sin; for his seed remaineth in him: and he cannot sin, because he is born of God'.

Many people at New Year's Eve make a resolution that they are going to change, but just turning over a new leaf will not be sufficient. You will not get a new nature just by doing this. We can attempt to be religious outwardly, we can start going to church or we can start reading the Bible but none of these things on their own will give us this new nature. In Matthew 5v20 it says that when looking into the hearts of the scribes and Pharisees, Jesus saw that they were only righteous on the outside. Their hearts had not got this new nature. It was all a show. This is why Jesus said that our righteousness should exceed theirs. For us to receive this new nature we have to make a true commitment to God and ask Jesus into our lives. In John 3v3-5 the Bible tells us that we must be "born again". This is a term that simply means that we have a spiritual experience with God. We are born of the flesh the first time, but there has to be a new birth that is of the spirit of God. This is a tremendous free gift from God. It can't be earned. If we could earn this then Jesus would not have had to come to earth or die for us upon the cross.

We can look around the world and put our trust in many other religions but Acts 4v12 says, 'there is no other name under Heaven given among men, whereby we must be saved'. No one else can set us free from the result of the fall. It's only through the blood of Jesus that we can be saved. Further proof of this can be seen in John 14v6 when Jesus said that He is the way, the truth and the life. No one can come unto the Father unless it is through him. We may think in our pride that we can earn God's respect and love by being involved in a charity or by convincing people that we have a kind nature. We may wear a red band around our wrist or even pray to gods that don't exist in the hope that we will enter a spiritual realm. The truth is, as we read in Ephesians 2v8-9, we can't save ourselves. We can't earn God's salvation. It's a free gift from God, but that free gift can only be received if we accept Jesus into our lives.

Chapter 4: Two Natures

When I was young my eldest brother had an old projector. It was nothing like modern day technology. The film reel would spin around making a noise and we had to use the landing wall at the top of the stairs to view the movie. This was the only free space in the house as every room was used by my sisters and their friends, and of course my parents had a big say as to where we could go. My eldest brother would point the projector at the top of the stairs as my other brother and I sat at the bottom waiting eagerly to watch his one and only film. We were always disappointed as his projector kept breaking down. We would sit in anticipation, for what felt like forever, waiting for him to fix it so we could watch the film. I don't recall us ever watching the entire film, I can only remember snippets.

The only film that he had was *Dr Jekyll and Mr Hyde*. In the film, Dr Jekyll invented a potion that could change his personality. He would take this potion and then he would wait as he began to feel the effects of the potion taking over. He would dive behind a desk, then after a short period of time he would reappear as a different person with a different character. This different character, known as Mr Hyde, would go on to do despicable crimes that Dr Jekyll would never have done. Mr Hyde went on to commit murder, which brought about his downfall.

Dr Jekyll and Mr Hyde is a classic story that reflects the two natures that dwell within each one of us. It reflects how we all can change from being a little angel one minute and into a raging monster that can't be controlled the next. We have all experienced something similar from time to time. It may have taken just one cross word or a strange look from another person and before you know it, and before you can stop it, you have changed into an angry person that you don't recognise. When you calm down afterwards you often can't believe what you have said or done. You often regret your actions but it's too late, the damage has been done.

The aim of this chapter is for us to get to know ourselves and find out what we are dealing with. I will try to show that these outbursts that affect us are the result of our own fears and insecurities that lie deep down within our unconscious. Even as Christians there will be times when we act more like the devil, when we show a side of our nature that is not Christ-like in the slightest. Like Mr Hyde we will say things and carry out actions that are most definitely contrary to God's Word. Then when we have calmed down we will wonder why we carried out such actions and said such vile things if God's Spirit is within us.

When these actions, words and thoughts invade our lives and we behave as if we have never known Christ, then there has to be a reason why we acted as we did. There has to be a reason why God has allowed this part of our nature to be revealed. To find out why we behaved like that we should turn to the Bible for answers. It can show us how we can deal with this sinful nature by confessing it to God and allowing Him to exchange it for His nature. It's important that we don't try to cover up what we have done or said as this will only make matters worse. It will only breed guilt. Our actions, however bad they may seem, should be brought into the light. They should be given to God and we should then wait for Him to show us the reasons why we behaved that way. Being honest gives God the opportunity to build upon the foundation that has already been laid through His blood that was shed for us.

1 Peter 1v15-16: 'But as he which hath called you is holy, so be ye holy in all manner of conversation; because it is written, Be ye holy; for I am holy.' Definitions of the word holy are pure, sacred, and clean. The meanings of the word holy reflect how we should be living our lives as Christians, so we need to ask ourselves the big question, 'Are we living this way in every area of our lives?' I don't just mean when we are out with our Christian friends or in church. I also mean when we are out on our own or in the privacy of our own homes. If we are honest I think the answer would be 'No'. Not because we don't want to do so, but because we have other thoughts and feelings that seem to rule our lives. We also have inner desires that rise up from out of the blue which we can't control. In our minds we are probably full of doubt and fears, not really understanding why we behave this way. We probably moan and complain, confessing anything but the truth. We may lie to others, ourselves and even to God, pretending that we are perfect. But what benefit will we

gain from doing this? The answer is nothing. It's much better to be honest and confess our faults then God can remove this side of our nature and exchange it for His own.

Jesus said that you can't serve two masters (Matthew 6v24), when he said this He was talking about serving God against wanting to be rich with the things of the world. He is not particularly talking about being wealthy, because Abraham was rich, as was Solomon. God blessed them both with vast amounts of riches, as he did with many others in the Old Testament. The truth that Jesus is trying to show us is reflected in what we waste our time building. Do we live for selfish needs, trying to build our empire, or do we live to serve God? I am not saying that we can't be wealthy. We can, but it's not our reason for living. Our reason for living is to know God and wanting to please Him. This is so different from the world's point of view where people are just living for self, where their whole lives are based upon acquiring wealth without a care for anyone.

In the Song of Solomon, we read about the bride's heart being a garden that is enclosed. It's a place where only

God was allowed to enter. It represents the part of us that is made especially for the Lord. Our heart belongs to God which means that it should not be filled with the concerns of this world. Our only desire should be to please Him and to find out what His will is for us. This doesn't mean that we are to be irresponsible with our finances. Neither does it mean that we shouldn't be grateful for all the things that the Lord does for us. Nor does it mean that we shouldn't enjoy life, or be friends with the people that we come into contact with. We can enjoy everything within reason that enters into our lives, but what we shouldn't do is allow them to come before God.

In our lives we should try to be good witnesses for the Lord so that His light can be reflected through us onto others. We should be trying to give them a glimpse of the living God. If our heart belongs to the world and we are only living for self then people will question our actions because, in their eyes, there is no difference between the way that we are living and the way that they are living. But if these people see that in your heart you have a special place that belongs to God then it makes the ones who hear His call to take note of your belief. But some will just ridicule you, saying that your actions prove nothing. No matter how you behave these people will still reject God.

The Word tells us that Jesus came to fulfil the law, but in the eyes of the scribes and Pharisees He broke the law. Jesus healed the sick on the Sabbath and His disciples picked ears of corn when they shouldn't have done. It was because of these actions by Jesus and His disciples that the religious orders of the day accused him of breaking the law. They had got so tied up with the written dead letter, that they had lost the very heart of the spirit of the law which was love. We can do this as Christians. We can grow proud and self-righteous in our interpretation of the Word, so much so that we can quote scriptures to keep people in bondage. We can interpret the Word in many ways, but before we condemn anyone let's remember Jesus said, 'he who is without sin, cast the first stone'. It's so easy to think that we are living our lives righteously before God, just as the scribes did, but it's important to remember that everyone walks a different path. We have to let God work the living truth in our lives as He does with other Christians. Then as this truth grows and our love for

God increases it will be easier for us to separate ourselves from corruption in the world. Our love for Him will be more important than anything else, but this doesn't just happen straight away. It happens gradually as our union with Him grows.

2 Corinthians 3v17 tells us, 'where the spirit of the Lord is there is liberty'. Liberty in this context means freedom to express the joy and love of Christ in every situation. Do we experience this liberty in our day-to-day lives, or do we walk around pretending to be righteous? People don't want to see others who act perfect and condemn others' faults. They don't want to see people who are lifeless, expressing no joy. When we behave in this way there will always be people who are looking to condemn Christianity. They will always be looking to knock you off the pedestal that you have put yourself upon. I am aware that some Christians act as if they are perfect because they want to please God and show Christianity in a good light. But their actions in the real world often have the opposite effect, providing ammunition to non-Christians, giving them the perfect excuse to reject Christianity. I am not saying that we shouldn't act righteous in front of friends and family but

the world needs to see real Christians who live their lives full of joy, who are full of liberty even if they make mistakes.

Making mistakes is an important part of growing up. This is how we learn right from wrong. It's a principle in the natural world and it certainly applies on our spiritual journey. Anyone who has ever made a mistake will remember that horrible feeling that we have inside as we try to fathom out how we managed to do such a stupid thing. Our pride is dented as the shock of our actions ripples down to the very foundation of our being. It's further damaged when we get abuse from our work colleagues and from the boss. If we are lucky and the mistake is not too damaging then we will just get a sharp reprimand. We will be shown where we went wrong and hopefully we will never make the same mistake again.

The mistakes that we make happen for a reason. They occur to show us our pride. They occur to show us that deep down within us there are areas that need bringing into God's presence. There is no shame in confessing that we have made a mistake. It's better to be honest and acknowledge our faults because God already knows what is hidden away from view. He knows that we are governed by fears. He knows we are proud and he knows that our actions are the result of our fallen nature rising up from our unconscious.

Many Christians believe that whatever they do in life is ok because as Christ's children they come under His banner and they could never imagine doing anything wrong. These beliefs come crashing down when they are having a bad day and one of their colleagues at work or one of their friends makes a remark that they don't like. As a result of their remarks the person is filled with anger and responds as never before. In their defence the Christian tries to make excuses. They blame others or circumstances to justify their actions but they fail to blame the true culprit i.e. themselves. By blaming others the perpetrator himself gets away scot-free and he has his credibility restored and he can resume his charade of being perfect. We may have fooled ourselves and others that the anger etc. was the result of other people's actions but we have not fooled God.

You don't have to teach children to lie, lose their

temper or to be selfish. They grow up with these things already within them. Most children grow up saying, 'I want this or that'. When their wishes are not granted they either act up to get attention or they use emotional blackmail. Either way, it's pride that is saying, 'I am here, give me what I want'. If we don't deal with this pride and deceit then Christians will behave in exactly the same way i.e. they will only go to God when they have a need or have a selfish urge that needs satisfying. They will only pray when they need healing or when they are in financial difficulty. Or they will try to blackmail God by saying, 'if you don't help me then I will never go to church again because you have let me down'.

From a young age people devise ways how to get away with doing bad deeds. Children will scratch and pinch their little siblings to get their own way. As the child develops and grows so does their imagination and it conjures up more elaborate plans to get their own way. Even though we pretend to be good in front of our family and friends we have a dark side to our nature that they know nothing about until things don't go our own way. If someone disagrees with what we believe, we will fall out with them even though we may have been friends for many years. When others question our actions and ask how we can behave like this, we try to justify our actions by saying it was God's will, but only prayer will show if this is really true.

It's with this deceitful nature that we plan how we are going to get our own way throughout our lifetime. We plot and scheme and invent stories and we truly believe that God is going to fulfil all our wishes. But as we walk with Him and we present our dreams before Him it seems that God has other ideas about where we should be heading. We have dreams of grandeur and wealth or big churches where we are going to be in the limelight serving God, but He doesn't seem to have the same plans as we do. In fact, He seems to block our plans and puts obstacles in our way.

When our dreams are not fulfilled it is normally because they were nothing to do with God. They were actually our dreams, but we added God's name in the hope that He would sanction them. Our deceitful nature still wants to be the centre of attention. Our ego still wants everyone to know who we are, even if it's hidden under the disguise of religion. When our plans go wrong, He tries to show us that they were coming from within our deceitful nature. These are the times when we get angry and we wonder why He has stopped our dreams from coming into fruition. There are many reasons why plans fail. It could be because of others or just simply because God doesn't want us to walk that path. The point is we will never know whilst we are angry, whilst we are blaming God. We need to ask Him where we are going wrong and what path we should be taking.

If we go to God in prayer and say, 'oh Lord why have you let this happen to me?' hoping secretly that God will hear our prayers and then change His mind, if we are hoping that God will feel sorry for us then this type of prayer is showing that our corrupt heart is still operating within us. It's still trying to get its own way. Prayer should be all about seeking to please God, seeking to find out what His will for us is and not what we secretly want.

When a person is 'born again' he cannot sin (1 John 5v18 and 3 John 1v11). This means that we are a new person. We have a new nature, and we have decided to follow a new path which is based upon new principles that belong to God. It's this new nature that cannot sin. It belongs to God who is pure and righteous. In 1 John 1v8-10 it says, 'if we say that we have no sin, we deceive ourselves, and the truth is not in us', which can make it very confusing if we do not know that we have an old nature still. Our new nature in Christ *cannot* sin. It was given to us by God when we accepted Jesus into our lives. The more we walk with the Lord, the more this nature becomes a part of us and it's this nature that will dominate our lives. In the last part of the chapter the verse is talking about our old nature that we need to reduce daily and it's this nature that *can* sin.

These two natures war against each other. The new nature wants to pray and study, but we will also be aware that there is a side to our nature that says, 'I will do it in a minute'. Which wins the battle depends upon how strong our will is at that particular time. If we have had a good day then the chances are we will want to either go out to celebrate or we will want to pray and study and share the day with God. If we have had a bad day then we will want to go out to cheer ourselves up or we will want to pray and study to find out why the day has not been so good. At first we find prayer and study exciting, especially when we've just accepted Christ into our lives, so we spend time worshipping Him. There's nothing else at this stage that we would rather do. God then begins to show us that this is just a phase that we are going through. It's not our original nature, which would rather be doing something else.

This battle between the two natures is one of the reasons why people turn their backs on God. He reveals to them that they have got to choose. They can either worship God with ulterior motives for the rest of their lives or, if they want a real relationship with God, they can be shown the areas of their lives that are full of deceit. God knows that our worship in the beginning has got a selfish motive, even though we are not aware of it at that stage. He wants us to worship Him, but He doesn't want it to be false. He demands that it comes from a true desire to know Him. The only way that God can show that our desire to worship Him is false is by placing us into situations that expose our true thoughts. This exposing challenges our belief and our faith and it gives us the opportunity to rebel and walk away or it deepens our union with Him.

At first God may use a simple test to see where our loyalties lie. It might be the night that we have set aside to search the Gospels. But when we arrive home from work we see in the TV listings that our favourite program is on at the same time. We decide that our study night can be put off this once and we will study tomorrow, but of course we never do. It may be that we are going to church one Sunday afternoon when suddenly out of the blue our friend pops around and says, 'we are just popping over to the pub, do you want to come out with us?' so we decide to miss church just this once. We assure ourselves it will never happen again, but of course it does.

Going to the pub with our friends or watching TV programs are not wrong in themselves but they are showing us that our old nature is at work. The choices that we make are revealing that our true desire is to be somewhere else. This might seem trivial but it's not. Gradually the desire to worship God will be lost and the desire to be a part of this world will take over. Although we will still be saved because we have asked Christ into our lives, we will have lost the chance to journey with the Lord, we will have lost forever the special times that we could have had in study, prayer and worship.

In the natural world man is making new discoveries every week. They are looking deeper into outer space than ever before. Man is shining a light into the darkest depths of the oceans as they try to unravel their secrets. Research into diseases that have never been conquered is having a huge impact as man tries to eradicate their influence upon the planet. Man on a natural level has never assumed that he knows everything that there is to know about our world or about the cosmos. He has always endeavoured to learn more, whatever the cost. The same should be true when it comes to knowing God.

2 Peter 3v17-18: 'Grow in grace and in the knowledge of our Lord and saviour Jesus Christ.' The reason that we are to grow in grace and knowledge is so that we are not led away in error with the wicked. These two attributes of knowledge and grace give us the perfect balance e.g. grace is not striving or struggling, it's realising that it's all undeserved favour that is freely being poured upon us by the tender love and mercy of God. We then have to grow in knowledge, first of all for

ourselves so that we will never be influenced by people with their own agenda. We also need to grow in knowledge so that we can share it with others. We can tell them of our experience and show them that they too are being called by God.

We need to pray and ask the Holy Spirit to make the Word alive and reveal Jesus to us in a greater way. Whatever is revealed to us we can thank the Lord for that truth and then commit it to Him, to work it in our lives. Even after salvation there is still work to be done within each one of us. We can't just sit back and think that we are pure or that we understand every aspect of God's Word. We are to press on with the calling from God.

The general belief when approaching the subject of salvation is that when God looks down upon us he now sees us through the blood of Christ and as far as He is concerned we are forgiven. We are a new creature and all things have passed away and our attitudes are changing just because we are Christians. This is what I was always led to believe. Christians could basically do whatever they want. Their actions and behaviour might be appalling at times but in the end they could rely on God's forgiveness. In some respects this is true. Nothing can ever separate us from God's love however we behave or however we react in certain circumstances. Undoubtedly there are many people who use this promise by God to carry on living just how they like. They act selfishly every day expecting Jesus to simply forgive them. To those who live their lives in this way I would say yes, you will be forgiven (although there will be some consequences to pay for your actions) but you will never grow in God's fullness.

When I was very young there was a nice young lady who used to walk along our street. Every time I saw her I ran up to her and asked if I could carry her bags. Everyone must have thought what a good little boy I was for being so kind. When I look back I wasn't being good at all. The reason I rushed to help her was because she would always give me a small treat. This was the true motive behind my actions. Even as Christians our good actions can have hidden motives e.g. we may decide that it would be a good gesture if we helped the old lady who lives just a few doors down our street with her shopping. We have seemingly good intentions and there doesn't seem to be anything wrong with our intervention. But if we brought these actions before God we may find that we are looking at a totally different scenario. When we bring our actions before the Lord in prayer or when we look at them in the light of the Word, to our surprise God will reveal thoughts and motives that we didn't know were there. He may reveal to us that our good intentions were tainted by selfish motives. He might show us that the reason we decided to help was just to show everyone what a good Christian we are. Maybe we wanted to impress our girl/boyfriend, or maybe you thought like me that there was a reward to be had.

One exciting thing about being a Christian is that God can help us to grow in any situation. He can show us new areas every day where our nature is not really what we think it is e.g. in our mind we may honestly believe that we are the most patient person in the world. Nothing seems to faze us; we take every situation in our stride. Then we come to a place in our lives when everything that we have ever known is turned upside down and the pressures of life begin to take their toll. Everything suddenly begins to get too much and we feel that we can't cope. With these building pressures we suddenly find that instead of being a patient person we become an angry person. We begin to shout and throw accusations at others. In this scenario God has revealed to us our true nature. He has shown us that our behaviour before was all a front. It was an act that we put on so that people would think well of us. We now have a choice. We can either blame all our anger etc. on others. We can say it was because of the pressure that we were under, or we can confess the truth and admit that this is the real us. If we follow the path that blames others then we will never grow and mature, whereas if we bow before the Lord and say, 'I didn't realise that these things were within me. Lord, forgive my impatience, anger, selfishness and pride. Take these out of my life, cover them with your precious blood and replace them with your nature of love, mercy and humility', then God will begin to remove this inner nature that is unlike Him. He will cleanse us and He will replace our dark side with His wonderful nature.

When Jesus walked the earth people didn't really understand Him. They screamed abuse at Him, but Jesus never showed impatience with them. His response was quite the opposite and He was moved with compassion. We can never be as perfect as Jesus but we can grow to be more like Him every day as we purify our old nature. We should never be downcast or feel guilty about what dwells within us. We just need to remember that we are human beings. We are not Jesus. He may have felt compassion but this doesn't mean that we always will. Some people are better at hiding their true feelings than others, so don't judge yourself by how others react. Their outward response may be very different to how they are feeling inside. When you read books about people who you thought were saintly, you will see that even they have had their moments when their actions were unlike Christ. They have been honest and written these occasions down for all to see. Most of the time they have been very Christ-like, but buried deep in their unconscious there was something that they were unaware of and God used a situation in their life to bring it into the light. This hidden nature that we all have has not taken God by surprise. He knew it was there all along.

If we are to be a light for the world around us then people have to see a change in our character. If we have spent our lives stealing from others and we continue to do so after we have asked Christ into our lives, then the people around you will totally denounce your Christianity as fraud. The reason that Christ came into the world is to set us free from how we lived before, and this changed life is what we should portray to the world. Our new life should be full of the joys that Jesus gives to us on a daily basis.

People today are always longing for what they know that they can't afford, or for an item that belongs to someone else. I have often been with my friends when a nice car has driven past and they say, 'I wish I had a car like that' or a nice girl walks into the office and they say, 'I wish she was my girlfriend'. This longing can often get us into trouble as can be seen by the amount of affairs that occur in the world today. We see on a regular basis marriage/relationship breakdowns because one of the partners has longed for someone else. We see people getting into debt because they longed to have the house or car that they couldn't afford. They get into debt to fulfil a dream but quite often their dream turns into a nightmare when they can't afford to pay back what they borrowed and they end up losing everything. Longing for things that we know we can never have can cause people to become depressed. I remember working with a man who fell in love with a friend's wife. He tried to win her over but when she rebuffed his advances he committed suicide. It was a shock to us all because no one knew the inner turmoil that he was experiencing.

These longings don't just go away because we are Christians. We too can be drawn into this world of desiring items that we know that we can't afford. We too can feel depressed when we don't have houses like our friends, or cars like our neighbours, or when we don't have the job that we have longed for all our lives. We know that these items are out of our reach, yet we still try to get God to give us what we desire. We pray, 'Lord help me out here, I need this car. I know it's expensive but I need it, I want it, please send along the money so I can have it'. When we pray this way we are really trying to blackmail God into giving us these things. We are hoping that this particular day God will be feeling generous. This longing is really coming out of this deceitful nature that I have been talking about. It may be our proud nature at work. It may be we fear losing other people's love because we aren't as wealthy as them. It's up to each individual to pray and ask the Lord, 'What is the reason for my longing? What am I trying to achieve through my actions? What are you trying to show me Lord?' It's important that we cleanse ourselves of these desires because of the damage they can cause. It's important that we stop desiring what we haven't got, and we focus more on what we have got in Christ.

When St Paul wrote his letter to the Hebrews (13v140) he stated that 'here we have no continuing city, but we seek one to come', in other words his eyes were fixed upon God and His kingdom. He wanted the people to follow the ways of Jesus. St Paul knew that this life was only temporary. He knew that riches and possessions would wither and die. He was more interested in being right with God and he was more interested in his eternal dwelling place.

If we could have this same vision of the eternal prize that St Paul had then we would be able to enjoy life more because we would not be worrying about wealth, houses or cars. We would fully understand that these pleasures are only temporary. Our joy would be in what lies ahead, when we are with God. Growing in the Lord on a daily basis will help us to attain this vision as we constantly shed our views of the world and we begin to focus more on God. We will then find that we are not living for selfish purposes, but we will be living to please God and be genuinely interested in others and how we can help them. Salvation is the most fantastic gift that we can receive from God. Jesus died in our place so that we can be in God's presence for eternity. Our sinful nature which would have been consumed in the fiery presence of God's purity is now covered with the blood of Jesus.

Chapter 5: God's headship over our lives

Throughout the whole of the Bible we see God's desire to be close to man. The scriptures tell us that even though man constantly ignores His love, God still holds out His hands with a welcoming gesture. Even when man rejected God's love at the birth of creation, even when God had no other choice but to remove man from His presence, God still provided an open door for man to return to Him. He has used physical signs such as the Tabernacle to open man's eyes to His truth. He has used His Word (the Bible). He's also worked through people's lives such as the prophets to reveal His desire for man. Finally, He revealed the greatest love of all through the death of His Son. Jesus was the ultimate revelation to man of God's love.

I think a lot of Christians fail to understand that, when they accept Jesus into their lives and they set off on their own spiritual journey, God is the guiding factor. Nothing in their lives will occur without God being head of it, whether it's something good like getting a new job or whether it's something bad like being seriously ill or not having enough money to buy the things we think we need. We have put our lives in his care, so we have to believe that he is going to lead us into the places where we need to be to find His will. One of the reasons why we don't believe this truth is because deep down in our unconscious is a little god that thinks that he is in control. This pride in our nature naturally thinks that we are in charge and when he can't control a situation he causes unbelief to rise to the surface. As we venture through the wilderness then God will show us how we can overcome this little god and put Him in charge instead.

Romans 8v28: 'we know that all things work together for good to them that love God, to them who are called according to his purpose.' This scripture in the New Testament tells us 'all things work together for good'. This 'all things' is a very important part of the verse to remember because it also includes the areas of our life that we inevitably think are bad. It includes the times when we are sad, depressed, when we think that we have lost all our friends, when our career prospects have taken a turn for the worst or maybe we break up with a loved one. It's in these times that God is leading us and if we seek Him then He will reveal important truths that will bring us closer to Him.

At the beginning of our journey our new found belief can seem very strange, simply because we don't fully know what is expected from us. Can a young man still look at a pretty girl as she walks past? Will God strike him down if he does? Will we ever taste a glass of beer again? Does God want me to still play football? All our thoughts are trying to adapt to a new way of thinking. We are born again into a new way of life where we are trying to make sense of all the truths that are coming our way.

We may be wondering what God thinks of us. Does He think that we are good people? Why is He bothering with the likes of me? When we look in the mirror we see a reflection that is nothing special. At this particular moment in time, we probably still think as the world thinks. We don't know all the scriptures. We are at a stage when we are trying to process all the information that we are receiving. We are being bombarded with testimonies, people telling us about their special relationship with Jesus. With all this information bombarding us it's easy to think that we have got it all wrong. Why does God need me? I will never be able to live according to God's Word. I will never be good enough to be a Christian.

Before we go any further I want you to take a long, hard look at Romans 8v28 because the emphasis is on 'to them that love God'. The scripture doesn't say 'to them who are perfect', or 'they have to be good looking', or 'to them who are clever or have loads of money'. We don't have to be anything special for God to love us. As long as we love Him and are trying to walk in His ways then He will use everything within his power to bring us closer to Him. In fact, 1 Corinthians 1v27 says that 'God has chosen the foolish things of this world to confound the wise'. So at the beginning of our journey we shouldn't worry about our mistakes. We shouldn't worry when our lives seem to be going in the opposite direction to that we thought we should be going. The only thing that we need do is trust God and asking Him to reveal His truth in whatever situation we find ourselves.

The way God operates to reveal His power and wisdom is often confounding to the world. In the eyes of man the world has to operate in a certain way. If it doesn't fit into our little box then it's either wrong or it doesn't exist. The miracles of Jesus are often questioned, even by Christians. They try to rationalise His actions and they come up with all sorts of answers as to how He performed them. According to some people, His actions are impossible to carry out. There must be a scientific explanation. They can't conceive that Jesus had power to manipulate the governing principles of our world.

The verses in 1 Corinthians 1v18-31 are talking about how people need a sign to believe. It's talking about how the death of Jesus upon the cross is a stumbling block to some and foolishness to others. But St Paul is saying it might seem foolish to man but God has chosen the foolish things because His foolishness is far greater than man's wisdom. Once again if man was involved, the whole scenario would have been so different. There would have been no way that the main character would have died and suffered a horrendous death. Jesus would have ridden into Jerusalem in power and glory, the Romans would have surrendered and their Empire would have fallen. But God's ways are not our ways, neither are our thoughts like His thoughts. The only way that we can return into God's presence is by believing that Jesus died for our sins upon the cross and through repentance.

Even if we decide to put our trust in God, why do we have to put our trust in Jesus? Jesus was a man who appeared on the scene about 2,000 years ago. He was born of Mary and Joseph and He grew up to be the greatest ambassador for God the world has ever seen. But Jesus was more than just a man. The following verses will show us that Jesus has always been around from the very beginning of creation.

John 1v1-3: 'In the beginning was the Word, and the Word was with God, and the Word was God...All things were made by him; and without him was not anything made that was made' It goes on to say in 1v4, 'in him was life; and the life was the light of men'. Later on in 1v14 it tells us that the Word was Christ Jesus. The Old Testament also refers to Jesus being there at the beginning of creation. It says in Proverbs 8v22-35 he was brought forth before the mountains and his delight was with the sons of men. Even before creation Jesus was there and he knew even then that one day he would have to come down upon this earth and die for us. This was the only way that we could return into God's presence and be part of His plan for us. If we put our trust in Jesus it means that we also trust the almighty creator to keep us safe.

As Christians we are called to be one with God and one with God's Word, which means we have to spend time reading the scriptures and then in prayer seeking God's guidance. As we do this on a daily basis we should become balanced. We should be able to judge what is right and wrong for us in our walk with God. If we don't become balanced then we can be led astray very easily and the race that we are called to run will end up being a stroll and we will not reach the finishing line to gain our prize.

As our knowledge of God's Word grows we will begin to understand how every small detail builds upon each other. We will begin to grasp how the Bible, even though it was written by many different authors, reveals one remarkable truth. The contradictions that everyone seems to highlight will come together as the Word reflects how God operates. The deep barriers that the scriptures seem to suggest will be removed and you will see the two sides of God's Word and how they fit perfectly together. The truths of the Word are like a diamond; it has many faces revealing the different aspects of God, yet it is one beautiful gem.

He wants us all to be a part of His master plan which Ephesians (1v10-11) informs us is 'when the fullness of times are completed God will gather everything back together in Christ Jesus'. God has called us to be a part of this restoration, to be a part of His will, when He restores everything back into balance. Ephesians 3v16-19 also sums up the reason we were created i.e. that 'Christ may fully dwell in us and that we may truly understand God's purpose, that we may enter into the love of Christ'. This is the pleasure that God was talking about in Rev 4v11. It's a love that we can't fully understand. It goes beyond our human comprehension. This is why St Paul prayed that 'we might comprehend what is the breadth, length, depth and height of God's love towards us', that we may see it in a greater and deeper way.

The best way to understand God's relationship with

man is through studying the scriptures, followed by prayer to allow the Holy Spirit to bring life into them. The Bible is full of stories that show how God interacted with man, but there are some scholars who say that these events never really happened. They say that there is not enough evidence to prove any of these stories. Some scholars go even further by suggesting that the great Kings of Israel, David and Solomon, never existed at all. The truth is that it doesn't really matter. What matters is the truth that those stories are trying to reveal to us when we pray over them. God has always used stories to portray spiritual truths. In Romans 1v20 it says that God always uses natural things to portray spiritual truths. The natural world and how we interact within it is a good way to show us what is happening in the spiritual world. Jesus used this way too. Just look at the stories He told through parables. He knew people could not understand the invisible truths of the Father, so he put the truth in stories.

In Ephesians 5v25-32 God shows us that He wants our relationship with Him to be like a perfect married couple, a true marriage union where everything is shared, even with his Church. Before man fell in the

Garden of Eden, Genesis 1v26 says, 'Let us make man in our image'. We were made in God's image which means that we were perfectly balanced. We were allowed to be in God's presence without any fear of being consumed. The reason for this was so we could know and fully experience God's ways and have a loving relationship with him in the same way a man has a relationship with his wife.

Being balanced brings about a loving relationship between God and man. In a loving marriage union a man and a woman come together. It normally results in them leaving everyone else behind as they set up their new home together. It's a union of love and surrender, of sharing and giving and from this union they often have children. So, in the spiritual way it's someone who loves God above all else. They have a desire for His will. They spend time alone with Him, getting to know Him and out of this loving relationship they bear the fruit of His nature. This is the union that God wanted with Adam and Eve. He wanted them to have His nature.

Once we have committed ourselves to this relationship God will keep us safe. If God has used all things to bring us to the place where we will accept Him as Saviour, how much more will He do to make sure that we have a chance of completing the greatest race of all? By accepting Jesus into our lives, we are saying that we want our nature to change. We are saying that we want God to be the head of our lives and we want to have this special relationship with Him. If we truly follow God and seek His headship then we will want to change our nature more than anything else in the world. It will be no surprise that as a result of our actions we can honestly say that as we walk with God our inner nature has changed. Admittedly, we are still not perfect and still make mistakes, but compared to how we used to live there has been a dramatic improvement.

According to Jewish teachings our Heavenly Father is known as the unknowable God. This is because however we try to describe His nature and who He is, we will always fall short of giving a true picture. We will always interpret our meanings with a limited mind and therefore we will never do Him justice. When Moses asked God, 'what shall I tell the Israelites when they ask me what is the name of the God that hath sent me?' God replied, 'tell them I am that I am'. The only way that we can get a small glimpse of the nature that God is trying to portray to us is through His name.

In Genesis 1v1 it says the name for God is Elohim which means Supreme God, from another word that means almighty, power, strong. The main principle that it conveys is to do with God's power and might. So it's saying that when God created everything He was using this part of His nature. He was the strong one, the mighty one that set things in motion. When God created man in Genesis 2v4 He uses a different name. This time he uses the name LORD God which to the Jews is known as YHVH and means self-existing or Eternal God. He is so tremendous that there is no way man can understand any part of Him unless He chooses to reveal Himself to us. When He does reveal Himself to us, He normally uses a side of His nature that we can relate to easily.

In a marriage there has to be trust. Both parties have to believe that the other has their best interest at heart. Adam and Eve were led to believe that God didn't want them to eat from the tree of knowledge because they would then be like Him. They were fooled into believing that God hadn't got their best interest at heart. The bride in Revelation has reached a different conclusion; she has come to realise that God is head over everything that she has ever done and He totally had her best interest at heart. She had learned to follow Him wherever He led her.

In the Song of Solomon, the relationship between the bride and her Lord is written down as a love song. Her heart is a place where the bridegroom can come and have this loving union with her. This has been His desire from the very beginning of time. When man was placed in the Garden of Eden He was showing that our hearts were at the beginning of a wonderful journey. They were placed at the centre of God's heart so that they could begin to grow in His nature.

Eden means pleasure and delight. God was showing man that they were in the very place where He could take pleasure and delight in them, and they could delight in Him. What a fantastic privilege this truth reveals, that man could be in the heart of God and actually know that we could give God pleasure.

When someone goes on a shooting rampage and kills

many innocent people, the question is often asked why God let it happen. Why didn't He stop this tragedy from occurring? The truth is He can't stop it from happening because He has given man free will to do exactly what he wants to do. This is the price we have paid for rejecting God in the Garden of Eden. We all have the power to choose for good or evil and it's up to us what actions we take through the course of our lives. Man was given this free will in the Garden of Eden. They were placed in an environment that reflected God's love. He gave man everything that he could ever wish for, but God also knew that if this two-way relationship was to be a real one then man would have to choose for himself whether he wanted to be a part of it or not. This is still the same choice that we all face today. Do we want God to be a part of our lives, and do we freely want to give Him our love?

Genesis 2v16-17: 'thou shalt surely die.' Adam and Eve were warned that if they chose to reject God's love then there would be a price to pay. This death wasn't referring to a physical death. They were in a spiritual realm at this point, so God was informing them that they would die spiritually and they would be separated from His presence. Through their choice man would also become mortal. They were forced out of the spiritual realms to become part of this world. Through Adam and Eve's choice to reject God we are all going to die a physical death, but we still have the choice before we die to accept God into our lives.

It has been a very long time since events unfolded in the Garden of Eden, yet God still calls us. He still wants to be involved in our lives. It breaks His heart to see people walking away from all that He offers, but He won't take away our free will to do so. He has given us the power to choose because He doesn't want robots who just blindly say, 'yes Lord, I love you, I want to follow you', when in actual fact we would rather be doing something else. God wants the special union that is talked about in the Bible of a Bride and Bridegroom relationship. The Bride is someone who has rejected all that this world offers. She will have been tempted by many things to reject God's call, but her desire to follow the Lamb wherever He leads has been stronger.

If we are to choose for God then we have to be aware that there are forces operating in this world that will do everything they can to stop you from answering God's call. In Genesis 2v15 it says, 'he put man in the garden to dress it and to keep it'. The word 'keep' means to guard, protect, beware, to act as a watchman. God was warning man that there would be an enemy approaching. If this was not the case then God wouldn't have told them to place a hedge around the Garden.

To keep our hearts safe from an attack we should surround it with God's Word. This will keep us safe from the serpent who tries to lure us away from God. We can see in the parable of the sower how easy it is to have the Word of God snatched away from us by the enemy. There are so many distractions in the world today that can cause us to forget what the Word says, so it's very important to pray over it and let the Spirit work it in our lives so that it can bear fruit. We can see this truth in Luke 11v28. It says, 'blessed are they that hear the Word of God, and keep it'. The bride in Revelation has found the Word of God so precious that she has kept it safe within her heart. It's an enclosed garden where only Jesus could walk.

In the beginning there was an angel called Lucifer, and

he was known as the Bringer of Light. When you read Isaiah 14v12-15 you will see that in his pride he wanted to be equal to God. He wanted to exalt his throne above the stars of God. But God could not allow him to remain in His presence so Lucifer was removed from Heaven, taking on a fallen nature as he fell from grace. It's with this fallen nature that he has attacked mankind since the dawn of time.

Satan is a powerful force of evil and he attacks our minds in a very real way. When we come up against a brick wall, this is Satan in our way. In 1 Thessalonians 2v18 St Paul wanted to visit his brethren but he says that it was Satan who hindered them. If Satan can stop you getting on in life then he will, especially if you are striving to know God as that's the last thing that he wants to have happen.

For the serpent to be able to put a fascination upon the Tree of Knowledge, he had to remove the very thing that God had given them to protect themselves, which was His Word. If only we would stay within God's Word then we would be safe, but so often we forget what God has said and this allows the serpent to put a fascination upon things that will lead us away from Him. The serpent is crafty and he comes along and the first thing he does is to sneer at God's Word e.g. 'does the word really say that?' or 'you don't believe that rubbish'. Then we start to give way to him and we start to think, 'maybe that bit of the Bible isn't true', and then we think, 'if that's not true then maybe that bit isn't true either' and, 'that bit certainly can't be true'. Before we know it, God's Word isn't surrounding us anymore and the serpent can tempt us to do anything. We are then in a vulnerable place. We are blinded from the truth which means that we will do something stupid without really thinking of the consequences. After the event our eyes are quickly opened to the truth of what we have done and we will find that we are in a mess. This is when he moves in for the kill and he begins to attack us with the other aspects of his fallen nature.

Romans 3v23: 'For all have sinned and come short of the glory of God.' Sin means to miss the mark, to forfeit, be led astray. Mankind has fallen a long way since the days when he walked and talked with God. Having had an eternal body we now have one that doesn't always function as it should. We have a body that is open to disease and as a result of now being mortal we die. On this earth our time is very limited and we never know how long we have to enjoy it because death can be waiting around the corner. Recently I have lost a number of friends and family members. I know their lives were very special indeed. They enriched all the lives of the people they came into contact with but unless there is an afterlife their lives would have meant nothing at all.

I know that some people believe that death is the ultimate end. They are adamant that there is nothing else. I am aware that there will always be people who have not heard God's call, people whose spiritual eyes will never be opened to see the wonders of God and His creation. As time passes and knowledge increases the serpent will have the opportunity to tempt people into enjoying their lives through other rewarding activities. As the desire to know God fades mankind will become more fascinated with the acquirement of riches, drugs, drink, science, astrology, spiritualism, lovers, anything that will lead them away from God. If we are to run the race that St Paul talks about, to reach the ultimate prize, then there should not be any room for these other things. This doesn't mean that we can't be involved with other activities but it means that they shouldn't take priority.

If we can be tricked into believing that these obsessions, desires etc. are more important than knowing God and we spend our brief spell of life without a thought for Him, then when our lives are over and we are placed in the ground or cremated then this is all that life was about. If this was the truth, what a sad end to our existence this would be. It's important to note that the serpent isn't just interested in separating you from God in this life. His main aim is to bring about the death that the Bible was referring to, which is being separated from God. If we look at the story in Genesis, this was the first thing that Adam and Eve encountered when they were put out of the Garden. Unless our eyes are opened to the truth then we will always be separated from God, not just in this life but throughout eternity.

John 3v16: 'God so loved the world that he gave his only begotten son, that whosoever believeth in him should not perish, but have everlasting life.' This shows the tremendous love of God, something that we can't ever truly understand. This is a fallen world that doesn't want to know God, yet He loves us so much that He sent His only son to die for us upon the cross. Jesus on the cross took all the pain and suffering that should have been ours and He triumphed over it. Isn't this a wonderful truth to behold, that in the midst of a world where everyone is only concerned with their own selfish needs, we have an eternal God who loves us so much that He is involved with every aspect of our lives? We may only think that He is with us when we are happy, when times are good, but this is far from the truth. He is also with us through all the troubled times that we may encounter. We may moan and complain more when life is not going our way because deep down our pride is telling us that we should never experience situations that cause us pain, but it's normally in these painful times that we are in fact closer to God.

Chapter 6: Into the wilderness

The Children of Israel's journey from Egypt into the wilderness shows how their story relates to our own inner journey with God, as we leave the life of bondage that Egypt represents to follow God into the wilderness where we encounter different experiences that shed light on our true self. In the two previous chapters we endeavoured to understand how our unconscious was still governed by a part of our nature that is only interested in pleasing self.

In this chapter we re-join the Israelites as they leave Egypt. They are led by Moses to the shores of the Red Sea where Pharaoh has the opportunity for revenge. In their hour of need God comes to their rescue sending a strong wind to part the Red Sea which allows them to pass over safely on dry ground to the other side. Their ultimate salvation came when Pharaoh sent his army in hot pursuit into the depths of the Red Sea. Their aim was to destroy the Israelites before they crossed to the other side but God had other ideas, bringing the water crashing down upon them. Having watched Pharaoh's army being destroyed, Moses and the Israelites had cause to celebrate before they eventually set off on their arduous journey into the wilderness.

We may wonder why the Children of Israel doubted God. They moaned and complained about the situations they were in. They experienced the waters of the Red Sea being parted. God went before them in a pillar of fire, and they had lived through all the plagues that had befallen Egypt. The truth is when we are in a situation that causes distress, we often fail to remember what God has done in the past. Our eyes are only focused on the here and now. These situations that God takes us through expose the real us and identifies areas that need dealing with and that need surrendering if we are to increase our union with God.

For those people who don't like the Old Testament stories, or choose to ignore them because they feel that the New Testament is sufficient to meet their needs, I would like to bring to your attention 2 Timothy 3v16 where it says, 'All scripture is given by inspiration of God, and is profitable for doctrine, for reproof, for correction, for instruction in righteousness'. We have to remember that when this letter was written it was referring to the Old Testament because the New Testament was not written down yet. Therefore we can conclude that the letter written to Timothy was indicating that the stories in in the Old Testament were given by God to reveal spiritual principles to all who delved into their meaning. If this is true then we can look at the Children of Israel's journey and use it as a blueprint of a well-worn path that we should walk. Their journey shows that there will be times when we have doubts and fears. It reveals that we will have to face many battles, winning some easily while other enemies will take longer to defeat. The scriptures also point out to us why some Christians find this journey too hard and why they long to return to their old way of life. The scriptures also reveal how we all at times lack faith to follow God wherever He leads us. The most important revelation that we can glean from all these Old Testament stories is that, in spite of all the downfalls, we see the faithfulness of God as He walks daily by our side.

When the magnitude of our decision to follow Christ sinks in, there will come a time shortly afterwards when we think to ourselves, 'What have I done? How am I going to explain this to everyone?' The little Pharaoh/ego that dwells within suddenly realises that he is going to be the centre of ridicule so he begins to send messages to our carnal mind questioning our decision. We will have thoughts such as, 'Have you thought this through?', 'Do you really believe what you have heard?' and, 'Are you willing to lose some of your friends?' On top of every negative thought that we are thinking, our friends are also asking questions. They can't believe that we have turned our lives upside down to follow this Jesus guy. We become the centre of their ridicule, or even anger at times, as they berate our decision. From the moment our feet begin to trace His footsteps we will always be tested as to who we follow. It's a continuous battle that lasts throughout our lifetime as the unconscious within tries to regain control over your life, while God seeks to expose our faults so that we will confess them to Him.

Exodus 14v5: Pharaoh said, 'Why have we done this, that we have let Israel go from serving us?' He has just realised what he has done. The Israelites will no longer be able to serve him if they leave Egypt to serve God. The Israelites may have been freed from Egypt, as we are now freed from our life of bondage, but our old self where Pharaoh/ego dwells will not give up his hold on us without a fight. Pharaoh will use everything within his power to get you to turn around. He will use every tactic that he knows to stop you developing as a Christian. In Exodus 14v6-9 it says that he gathered all his chosen chariots and men together and he set off to stop them from leaving. These chariots and men represent our best excuses that we have. These handpicked chariots are chosen because Pharaoh knows that they can get the job done. He hopes that their swift attack will kill off any ideas that we have of following God and we will quickly be under his control once more.

Our unconscious quickly sends out all these excuses as to why we shouldn't follow God. He wants to stop us in our tracks before we can take things any further. With all these thoughts whirling around our minds, God leads us to the place where He wants us to face up to Pharaoh. It's probably a time of confusion. Pharaoh seems to have the upper hand. As he approaches with his mighty army we can see in v10 that the Children of Israel were afraid. There will come a point in our lives when Pharaoh's army seems almost invincible. It will seem that we have no other choice but to return to the land of bondage. If we don't return then we fear that we will somehow cease to exist, our friends will forsake us and our own sanity may never be the same again. This is the biggest decision that we will ever make. As Pharaoh draws near to the part of us that is looking to escape the bondage of Egypt, the fear will increase. There is no escape; we are hemmed in on all sides. Which way do we turn? We have to make a choice. Do we follow God, or do we give in to Pharaoh? It's a very scary situation to be in, but everything rests on our free will choice.

In Exodus 14v11&12 we see the turmoil going on within us. There is a part of us that wishes we had never left the land of Egypt and all its comforts. Our old nature is saying deep within us you should have left us alone to serve the Egyptians. We were happy there and we wouldn't be in this mess now if you had left us there. On the other hand in v13&14 we see the new nature, the side of us that has chosen for God, saying be still and see the salvation of the Lord. It will also be saying to our old nature hold your peace, God will fight for us, God will set us free. When we start on our journey with the Lord we will probably have a lot of preconceived ideas. We may think that God is going to give us an easy life and that we will never encounter any more problems and life is now going to be full of joy. How wrong can our preconceived ideas be? Yes, we will have times of great joy and know that God is always with us, but our walk with the Lord will also be one of conflict where we have to make some very difficult decisions. One of those hard choices is right at the start. Do we give in and go back to Egypt, or do we press on with God to the Promised Land?

Which choice we make may come down to how much we want the Lord to be a part of our lives and how much we believe His Word to be true. In Matthew 13 when Jesus was telling a parable about the sower He revealed that some seeds fell by the wayside, some on stony places, some fell among thorns, but some seeds fell on fertile ground. The sower was throwing his seeds (which reflect God's Word) onto the earth in the hope that some would take root and grow. Jesus reveals that when His Word is shared there are always people who make excuses not to follow Him. Some people start off believing but when the going gets tough they go back to how they used to live. On the other hand there are some people who hear the Word of God and will follow Him wherever He leads because their seed landed on fertile ground. It says that some grow thirtyfold, some sixtyfold and some one hundredfold. How much we grow depends on how much we want to follow Him. To those that fully mature and have changed their nature totally, they will grow one hundredfold. For those that truly believe that their choice to leave their old way of living was the right decision will, when Pharaoh comes along with his mighty army of excuses, ignore him and move to the next stage. They will continue to follow God.

This next stage can be seen in v13 when Moses says unto the people, 'Fear ye not, stand still, and see the salvation of the Lord, which he will show you this day'. To stand still means that we are not running to and fro, trying to get everyone's opinion on the matter. Neither will they be afraid of all the arguments that Pharaoh tells us. We will be calm and listen to the small voice of God that is quietly telling us the truth. It's only when we are still that our hearts and minds will be in the right frame of mind to hear what God is saying. If we are troubled within then we will never hear what God is asking us to do to be set free.

Moses used his rod to cause the waters to return to their full strength. It was this action that destroyed the Egyptian army. This is showing us that our old ways of living can never be a part of our new spiritual life. They have to be killed off. Once we have made the decision to follow God then we should never want to return to how we used to live. We are told that we are to live in the world but not to be a part of it. God wants us to enjoy all things but we are never to be so joined to them that we could never give them up if God asks us to do so.

In Exodus 14v26-31 on reaching the far side, the Children of Israel realise that the Egyptians who once totally ruled their lives are now gone. The dead bodies of Pharaoh's soldiers lie floating in the water or they are washed up on the seashore. They are there as a reminder of what life used to be like, but it also reveals the future to the Israelites that they are now free to follow God. One of the reasons why we never leave Egypt is because we can't imagine ourselves being separated from the life that we enjoy. We can't imagine not going to the pub, or going to nightclubs. We can't imagine ourselves never gambling again or never taking drugs again. When God sets us free it's like having our eyes open for the first time and we really see these habits for what they are and we wonder how they ever managed to keep us in bondage.

Although the Egyptians are dead they are certainly not forgotten. Just like any bad habit we will have urges to return, but as we grow in the Lord these urges will gradually fade until they are a distant memory. At this stage of our spiritual journey we don't fully understand what is expected of us so when the going gets tough we tend to seek the comfort of what we know. Ahead of us lies a journey into the unknown. It's here where we will face many conflicts and we will have to make some serious choices as to who we are going to serve. When we are making these choices it's good to remember that we have been set free by the cross of Jesus and He will provide the things that we need to survive any wilderness experience.

Exodus 15v1: 'Then sang Moses and the children of

Israel this song unto the Lord.' After the Children of Israel had seen the great works that God had done and they were safely on the other side, they began to sing and praise the Lord. When He sets us free from our old nature that was keeping us in bondage, there is an inner joy that explodes inside that makes us want to praise God for all He has done. The only comparison that I can think of is a person who has been blind all their life having an operation to restore their sight. When they come round after the operation and have the bandages removed, imagine how they must feel when the first flickers of light flood into their eyes and they can see for the first time. This is what it is like to become a Christian who no longer walks in the darkness of this world but experiences God shining into every dark recess that we have in our unconscious, uncovering the dark secrets that kept us from Him.

Let us resume our journey in Exodus 15v22 where it says they left the Red Sea and moved on into the wilderness. They left the initial place of their euphoria and travelled deeper into the wilderness and it says that they found no water. Then in v23 it says that they came to Marah, but the waters were bitter and they could not drink it. Many Christians find it hard to drink the waters that God offers because they are always comparing them to the waters that they have tasted in Egypt. The River Nile brought life to the surrounding area and we can relate this flow to meeting our inner desires such as going to the pub or discos. For some it's taking drugs. For the younger generation it probably represents spending hours on computer games. in fact it can represent anything that we do that is pleasurable to the little ego that dwells inside us.

The water that God is offering us is totally different because it is not based on just living for self, it's based upon knowing God and this is why it seems so bitter. To the world, the waters of Christianity are boring. People don't want to spend all their lives going to church, praying or reading the Bible. They want the excitement of Egypt. They want to experience the hustle and bustle of the world. Walking with God takes us away from this type of life. Instead of seeking outward pleasures God takes us on an inward journey where we learn to find our true selves. If Christians are not informed that the waters of God are different from Egypt then their expectations of what God has to offer can often be a let-down and can cause them to walk away from what God is offering.

They then hover between the two worlds, never really committing to either. They will always look for someone else to blame, as we can see in v24 when they blamed Moses, but really it's showing that they have not fully grasped what God is calling them to do. If we are to follow God then we have to take responsibility for our own actions. This is the inner struggle that we all face. This is how we grow in the Lord, through rejecting the pull of Egypt and all its offerings and putting our trust in God that He will give us the true waters that bring eternal life. We have to understand that from now on the waters that we drink belong to God. Jesus said that He is the water of life and it's only by knowing Him that our thirst can be quenched. If we want to taste the waters of Egypt then we will never be satisfied. We will always want more. This is why people today are always looking for the next kick. They move from one addiction to another in the hope of being satisfied, but they never are.

In v25 it says that Moses cried unto the Lord, and that

'the Lord showed him a tree, which when he had cast into the waters, they were made sweet'. What a fantastic truth this is! The tree portrays the cross of Christ. Grace flows down from God and sustains us so that any bitter situation that we may face can be made sweet by Him. When we throw the cross of Christ into any situation we will find forgiveness. We will find that God will give us the answers. He will be everything that we need and we will come to realise it's the waters of Egypt that are bitter because they only bring death. Jesus is the true water of life that will sustain us for eternity, but unfortunately people don't see this. They are only interested in the here and now. The ironic part is that everyone is looking for the next high because, deep down without them even realising it, they are looking for the union that they once had with God right back in the Garden of Eden.

If we are to remain in God's presence then our eyes have to be opened. God wants us to recognise these well-worn inner beliefs and fears that we have and He wants us to bring them all before Him so that they can be cleansed and washed out of our lives for good. So many Christians brush the way they behave under the carpet pretending that their inner house is clean. They present a spotless front door and lovely curtains for the world to see, but if you walked into their house (unconscious) you would find something very different. God wants us to see our inner house for what it is and He wants us to confess what lies within, from the pride in the attic to the bad habits concealed in the basement. He wants to remove all the rubbish that we have accumulated over the years.

At salvation God enters our house and dwells in the living room. At first this is the only place where we have given Him permission to walk. The rest of the house is out-of-bounds. It's hidden away, full of dark secrets. As our love for Him grows we give Him permission to enter these dark rooms and His light reveals that we are bitter about many things that have happened over our lifetime. His light shows us that locked away in one of the cupboards is a packet of anger that still influences our relationship with people. Under the stairs is a bad memory of when we were younger. Instead of confronting it we hid it, hoping that it wouldn't be able to hurt us ever again. On the basement door His light reveals a sign that says, 'do not enter'. This is the area that we hoped the Lord would never see. We thought we could follow Him without Him knowing our desires or our dark thoughts that we keep hidden away.

The truth is God already knows what we have hidden away. He knows every aspect of our house intimately. He wants us to say, 'Lord, even though I know that there is a part of me that wants to return to Egypt, I choose to follow you. Forgive me for having these desires and give me your nature to replace mine'. Exposing the dark secrets of their inner house and getting them to repent over the way these areas influenced their walk with God was the only way that the Children of Israel could be healed. If we try to keep the dark side of our nature hidden away then it will always try to influence our walk with the Lord. It will always rebel against God when He leads us into situations where we need to learn humility. God may want us only to drink the waters of Marah that may seem bitter, but our pride will be telling us that we are worthy of Champagne.

We all have different beliefs, different doubts and fears and many other psychological factors that can influence the way that we behave. If we don't deal with them by confessing the way we feel to God then they can grow and become the dominant factor in our lives. They can also remain dormant for many years then all of a sudden someone will say something and this anger that has been hidden away will erupt out of control. Our witness to God is blown and the worst case scenario is that we blame God for what has happened and we end up returning to our old way of life because we believe God has let us down.

Growing into His nature is an important part of the process. We can see in the scriptures written down that the Children of Israel's journey can be divided into three stages. We first of all encounter God in Egypt where we freely choose to follow Him. From this place we venture into the wilderness where God exposes our weaknesses and our longing to return to Egypt i.e. the life we have just left. Finally, we are allowed to enter the land of Canaan, the place where God has promised us milk and honey.

Through each stage God places us in certain situations that reveal our deep hidden thoughts. He exposes areas in our life that we didn't even know were there. He brings them to the surface to see if we are willing to confess them to Him. For example in stage one we have to admit that we are a sinner and we have to accept Christ as Saviour. If we don't then we will always remain under the influence of Egypt. For those that accept God's forgiveness and move into stage two, the journey into the wilderness, the battles that they have to face are totally different from the battles of Egypt. If the people who enter into the wilderness never really overcome these battles in the desert then their attempt to enter into Canaan's land will be thwarted. They will either die wandering in the desert or they will return to Egypt. Those allowed to enter into Canaan's land will have to face even tougher battles. They will have to drive out the tribes that have inhabited the land for a long time.

When God first told the Children of Israel to enter the land of Canaan, their response was to send twelve spies into the land to view it and to report on what they saw. Out of the twelve spies only two recommended that they should enter the land because their faith was in God. The other ten reported that the land was too great for them to enter. As a punishment for their lack of faith in God, everyone above the age of 20 who were not willing to enter because they feared what may happen to them had to die. We might think that God was not very merciful, but God was really showing us that if we want to be fully one with Him then we have to face up to and confess the way we are feeling. These doubts and fears have to be removed from our unconscious. They have to be killed off. These stories are valuable lessons that we must learn if we are to progress. They are not written down to put us off. Quite the opposite, they are written down to encourage us on our journey. God loves us so much that He has made provision for us through these stories to reach the very heights where we can be one with Him.

We live in a world where people expect everything to be provided. If we have no money then we expect the government to intervene. If we have no food then there are charities that will help. Whatever our particular need is, we expect it to be met. If our needs are not met then we look for someone to blame. It's got to be their fault that we are short of that particular commodity that we need right now. If we are honest and look into our own natures then we will see this is true. We moan and complain about everything and everyone and it's all because we have this proud nature that thinks we are the centre of the universe and the world should revolve around us.

It's good to recall at this point that we are dealing with the two sides to our nature. We have the old nature that is full of pride who tells us that we are worthy of more and wants all the luxuries of Egypt. It's this side that blames God and say it's His fault that this is happening. Moses represents the spiritual side of our nature who is trying to lead us to a better life with God. It's this side of our nature that will take the problem to God and ask for His guidance. Whichever side of our nature that we listen to will indicate to God whose will we are seeking to please e.g. if we are listening to the old nature/ego that is moaning and complaining and is blaming others then we are seeking our own will. If we take the problem to God then we are seeking His will.

Although God will not intervene He will try to show man through everything that goes wrong in the world that they need Him in their lives. He tries to show man that the lie that they accepted at the fall, that they can be as God, is not true. Man is weak and is subject to the laws of nature. When we accept God into our lives, He will use disasters that we experience in exactly the same way. He will show us how weak we are. He will show us how much we need Him in our world. Everything that occurs in our lives can be used for good or for evil. It can be used as an excuse to blame God or it can be used to see how much we need Him. We can use every situation as an excuse to blame others or we can see it as an opportunity to reveal an aspect of our nature that is unlike His.

Exodus 17 v8-16: 'Then came Amalek, and fought with Israel in Rephidim.' Have you ever wondered why the Bible verses seem to jump from one story to another without really explaining why? We have the Israelites coming to Rephidim and finding no water. We suddenly jump from the water scenario and then we have 9 verses that recall their encounter with Amalek as the two sides battled it out. When this battle is finished chapter 18 begins with the reappearance of Jethro. Were the authors completely mad to write this way or were they inspired by God? Was God, through them, trying to show us the complexity of our human unconscious, revealing how our actions are not something that occur on a random basis but they are the result of deeper activity in our unconscious that God wants us to deal with?

Let me try to explain why Amalek suddenly appeared on the scene ready to do battle. Every tribe that the Children of Israel encounter on their journey and face in battle represents a deeper force that lurks in our unconscious. These forces lie in wait, ready to pounce when they see any signs of weakness within our spiritual camp. The Amalekites would have been watching the Israelites from a distance and when they saw their actions over the water they would have taken it as a sign that the Children of Israel were in disarray and they took their opportunity to attack.

The Amalekites, who were a warlike people, dwelled in the valleys and were known as the men of caves. When relating this to our old nature it is showing that the first battle that we will face is to do with our base nature. Amalek was the grandson of Esau and therefore the natural enemy of Jacob, the rightful heir of God's promise. The Amalekites had waited for many years to take their revenge, and as soon as the Israelites had left Egypt they were ready to pounce.

I am not going to go into the complexities of the battle and the hidden meanings that surround it. I will leave you to pray to the Lord and ask him to reveal them to you. The point that I am trying to reveal to you is that when we become Christians we will encounter forces from within like the Amalekites who represent the undisciplined base nature within us. These forces will try to destroy your new life with the Lord. We may not think that there is anything within our old nature that would attack God's authority over our lives, so it's important to recall that the Amalekites had been waiting a long time to get revenge; they had been waiting in secret.

It was the Israelites' moaning and complaining that gave Amalek permission to rise up. God knew that the Amalekites lay in wait. He knew that they would attack given the chance so He manipulated the whole situation to reveal that they were there. He knows that if we are going to grow and mature and enter Canaan's land then this side of our nature has to be killed off. It is interesting to note that the Hittites, Hivites, Jebusites, Amorites and Canaanites who were major players in that region decided at this point not to enter the fray. They were hoping that the Amalekites could defeat the Children of Israel on their own. All these tribes represent forces and old habits within our unconscious. They are major players and influence our every move but on this occasion they remain hidden away from view. Some of these forces and habits are too powerful for us to deal with at this stage of our spiritual growth, but as we grow and mature then God will cause these armies to cross our path. When He reveals them to us then we have to be willing to face them head on in battle.

We have to remember what the Word of God says about our heart. In Jeremiah 17v9 it says, 'the heart is deceitful above all things, and desperately wicked: who can know it?' The whole reason the Amalekites and other tribes are revealed is to show us how deceitful we really are. God wants us to realise that we have a major battle on our hands if we are to follow Him through the wilderness, and even greater battles lie ahead when we mature enough to enter Canaan's land. All these encounters can seem very daunting as they entail dealing with areas of our life that we didn't even know existed. Our reassurance lies in how the Israelites won their first encounter. They achieved victory because God was with them. Without Him the task would be too great. When Moses lifted his hands the Israelites were successful, but when he lowered them the Amalekites prevailed. This portrays lifting the Lord up when we are facing the enemy. He is the only one who can give us victory. He is the only one who can set us free. If we look through the verses of the Bible we will see that every time the Children of Israel went into a battle with God in charge they never lost, but when they attempted to defeat their enemies without him then they were badly beaten.

There is also a warning in v16 where it says that 'the Lord will have war with Amalek from generation to generation'. Some forces within us are so deep that we may have to face them many times before they are overcome. So just like Moses, we should just build an altar to the Lord and thank the Lord for his support to overcome the portion that has been revealed. We then have to leave the whole situation with God until the next time it is revealed to us.

When the Israelites dwelt in Egypt they would have looked up in awe as they gazed upon the palaces, treasure cities and of course the Pyramids. But the greatest thing they would have hoped to have seen would have been a glimpse of Pharaoh. Even though they did not worship Pharaoh as a god, it would have been a tremendous privilege to be in his presence. Deep down we think that it is a privilege for people to know us, to be in our presence. Our ego thinks that people should stand in awe as we walk by.

All this changes when we come into God's presence. When God descends into our world it shatters this illusion that we once had about ourselves, and it can be quite scary. In Exodus 19v16 it says that there was thunder and lightning, and a thick cloud upon the mount. And the voice of the trumpet was exceedingly loud, so that all the people that were in the camp trembled. If we are to be humble enough to walk in God's presence then our pride has to be shattered. We have to realise that we are worthy of nothing. We have to take on the nature of Jesus. He was King of Heaven yet He was willing to humble Himself.

Exodus 19v17: 'Moses brought forth the people out of the camp to meet with God.' Once again we see the difference between someone who has grown and matured in the Lord, and someone who has just begun their journey. When someone new comes into the Church they have to rely on the spiritual leaders like Moses to lead them to the place where they can encounter God. This would either be through the Word or through prayer. It's interesting to note that at this stage of their growth the Israelites are only allowed to venture so far, they are not allowed 'to go up into the mount or even touch the borders'. The punishment for their disobedience would be death. God knows that if they enter the mountain and stumble into His presence then they will be consumed.

Moses on the other hand portrays the mature Christian, someone who has fully changed his nature to be one with God. His growth, which has taken many years to achieve, allows him to walk upon the mountain and it allows him to be able to enter into God's presence. In v20 it says, 'the Lord came down upon Mount Sinai, and the Lord called Moses up'. The Lord then tells Moses in v21 to 'Go down, charge the people, and lest they break through unto the Lord to gaze, many of them will perish'. God can only give us revelationsGo according to our growth.

In v22-24 we are told that even the priests were not allowed to go as high as Moses, but they were allowed to go further than the Israelites. Without spiritual growth we won't be allowed to experience the very heights of God. We will be restricted, not because God doesn't love us but it's out of His mercy. He knows that the Israelites would have been consumed because their nature was still like wood, hay and straw, whereas Moses' nature was like gold, silver and precious stones (1Corinthians 3v12-13). It goes on to say that every man's work shall be revealed by fire. The more we grow the more we will be like God. It's this growth that will allow us to enter into the fiery depths of God's nature and not be consumed.

Exodus 20v18-21: 'They said unto Moses, speak thou with us and we will hear, but let not God speak with us, lest we die.' After hearing the thunder and the noise of the trumpets and seeing the lightning, the people have come to the conclusion that God is all-powerful and all-consuming. They realise that it would be a big mistake at this stage of their growth to bring their proud nature directly to Him. So they ask Moses to seek God's will on their behalf because they know that he is one with God and he can enter into God's presence to hear the truth. Our unconscious is starting to understand that if it is to survive it has to become one with God. But it knows that if our ego was presented before God at this stage then it would be consumed because it's still full of sin.

Having committed our lives to Christ, there will come a time when we realise that we want nothing else in our lives but God. We may enjoy other things but finding God's will is all-consuming. When we reach this stage in our lives, our ego will finally submit. It will from now on gradually begin to hand over the reigns to God. Our ego realises he can't stand before God himself because he would be consumed so he decides that it's time to listen to the spiritual side of our nature i.e. Moses. He represents the part of us that only wants to serve God and fulfil his will. It's the side of our nature that realises that life without God is pointless. It's the fulfilled part of our lives that is drawing closer to God every day. It's the new nature within that is able to enter into God's presence.

Chapter 7: God's provision for his people

One important factor that we can't ignore as we mature and grow old is the fact that we will all change. I recently went to a school reunion to see my old friends. As I walked in I was greeted by smiles from people that I didn't recognise. I smiled back hoping that as my gaze lingered upon their faces I would get a glimpse of who they used to be. It was only as the evening progressed and the conversation flowed that gradually the young people that I used to know came to the forefront and little traits that I remembered were still a small part of them.

The ageing process isn't the only part of us that changes. Our thoughts, beliefs, friends, the areas where we grew up and the partners who we thought that we were destined to be with forever all change. Everything about us changes. Everyone wants a new car, a new house, and the curtains and décor of our houses are changed constantly. Hairstyles, fashion, the shoes we wear, the places we go for our holidays...the list could go on and on. There is not one thing in this world that remains the same throughout life, except for God. His love for each one of us never changes. His desire for us to be one with Him will last throughout eternity, never wavering. This desire that He has to be a part of our lives has been written down in the scriptures. Although we live in a world that is full of change, when we read the scriptures one thing that we can be sure of is that God never changes in what He is revealing to us. The principles are constant all the way through the Bible from the Old Testament to the New Testament.

We seem to be living in a wishy-washy world where people often say that the Church has got to move with the times. What they are really saying is that God has got to fit into their way of living and their way of thinking. If He doesn't then they are not going to bother with Him. It might come as a shock to realise that we are the ones that were created. We are the ones who should fit into God's way of thinking, not the other way around. When we become Christians our whole aim should be to seek God's will through prayer and study, finding out where our lives might be displeasing to Him. We should want to grow into the full stature of Christ by changing our nature daily to be more like His.

After the Israelites were set free from the bondage of Egypt, God provided everything that they would need to fulfil their journey so that they might go on to worship Him in a greater way and grow in their relationship with Him. The Children of Israel's journey wasn't an easy one but on their way God made provision for them in many different forms. On leaving Egypt they were led by a pillar of cloud and fire, the Red Sea was parted, water appeared to them out of the rock and they were given the Ten Commandments. If we are called to grow then these scriptures surely must have been written down to show us important principles. If we study and pray over them, then they must reveal important truths about our relationship with Jesus and how we can grow closer to Him.

Hosea 11v1: God says, 'I have called my son out of Egypt'. We are all called out of Egypt to journey to Canaan's land where we can have a special union with Jesus. The promise to the Israelites was that they were going to be led to a land that was flowing with milk and honey. This was going to be a place where they could have a special union with God. If this was the promise then and we believe that God never changes, then this promise still exists today for all of those who have given their lives to Christ. This land portrays the relationship that God wants with us. It's the reason that Jesus died for us upon the cross. If we are feeling that our lives have never really moved on since salvation, if we feel that we would like to move on in our limited, besieged life and know more of God but we don't know how, then we can begin by reading God's Word and seeing how much provision there is for us, just waiting to enter our lives.

The stories in the Old Testament can give us encouragement because they can reassure us of God's greatness, even when the Israelites were seemingly at the brink of destruction. Sometimes it may seem that the enemies we face are too great to overcome. We may feel that God has let us down, that He has promised us the earth and then abandoned us. Once again the Old Testament can encourage us when we feel this way. God didn't promise the Israelites the chance to enter into Canaan, just to abandon them when the Amorites turned up. Whatever we are facing God knew it was there waiting to do battle with us. He knows that deep within us we have issues that need dealing with. If we choose to ignore these areas then they could be a hindrance further down the line and they could stop us from reaching our own Promised Land.

Not only will we have to face up to these problems physically, we will also have to face up to the psychological problems that they bring. For some it can seem like these battles have been there forever. Whatever we have to face in life, God will use it for our growth. We just have to be brave enough to face it head-on and trust in God.

In the natural world battles are never easy. They often result in many deaths and casualties on both sides. But when we fight spiritually there is a difference. The only casualties are the crutches that we thought we needed to enjoy life. God takes them away, telling us that we don't need them anymore. We no longer need other people's approval. We no longer need drugs or that cream cake to feel happy and loved. Our deceitful nature is cleansed and our peace comes about because of Jesus.

This principle can be seen working as the Children of

Israel ventured through the wilderness. They were gradually separated from their old way of life, their doubts and fears faded until finally they entered into Canaan. Once in the land they were portrayed like a wife being prepared for her husband. Having entered the land of Canaan their struggle to reach full maturity wasn't over. There were still plenty of battles to fight, not only in the land but they also had to fight other nations who had different beliefs. This is still true today. We not only have to wage war against our old nature and its desires, but we are surrounded by people who have other gods. They want to replace the one true God and establish their way of life on anyone that believes differently. Christians are constantly being bombarded on all sides to walk a different path, to include another god, to worship another idol. They are being told that it's all right to do so, but it's not. If we are to reach the prize that St Paul talked about then we should never entertain these other worldly gods because they are simply distractions that will lead us away from God.

Ezekiel 16v29-32: 'But as a wife that commiteth adultery.' When the Israelites put other gods before the Lord they were seen as adulterers. We simply cannot have other gods in our life. We have to have a change of heart and put God first, even though it may be a very difficult thing to do. It may mean giving up gambling, drugs or drinking. Whatever it is God will show you and give you the strength. The point that I am trying to make is that your life may seem to get worse, and the Word will bring conflict to your life. We can see this truth in Exodus 5v21-23. First of all everything seems to get worse for the Israelites. Even Moses gets angry with the Lord because it's not working out like he thought that it should. Moses and Aaron speak to Pharaoh and he makes things harder for the Children of Israel, which causes them to blame Moses and he then blames God. Our faith will constantly be tried to see who we are putting our trust in. The only truth that we can be sure of is that Jesus will be with us every step of the way, leading and guiding us, revealing His truth and helping us to overcome major obstacles.

Chapter 8: Seeds of life

When reading the stories in the Bible we might mistakenly believe that it's normal for God to reveal Himself through a burning bush, a pillar of smoke or fire, through angels or maybe through a flaming chariot. We may be wondering if God revealed Himself to certain people in this way before, why isn't He revealing Himself to me in this way now? The scriptures in the Bible indicate that God interacted with many different characters in a special way e.g. St Paul experienced Christ in a blinding light. Mary encountered Archangel Gabriel when she was told that she would give birth to Jesus. In the Old Testament the scriptures tell of the special relationship Elijah, Abraham, Enoch and many others had with God. We read that Moses ascended Mount Sinai to meet God, whereas Adam walked and talked with God in the Garden of Eden.

It would be awesome if we woke up every morning to have an encounter with angels, or if we looked out of our bedroom window to see a pillar of fire gliding majestically around the corner. But the truth is these encounters were not an everyday occurrence for these people. Although sometimes there are only a few lines or chapters between their encounters which makes it seem like they were constantly meeting God, in actual fact they would go years without hearing a peep from Him. In the years in between their encounters they had to live by faith just as we do. Every day they probably wondered what God had in store for them, wondering if this was the day when God would reappear and interact with them, but until He did they lived their lives the best way they knew how.

I'm not saying that we can never experience the presence of an angel or even see one because I know people who are far more spiritual than I am who have told me that they have seen and met angels, and I know from my own experience that God reveals Himself through the Word and through prayer. What I'm saying is that God is with us every day of our lives and He speaks to us in many different ways but we shouldn't expect Him to appear to us in a blinding flash of light. We shouldn't expect Him to call us up a mountain or suddenly appear in a burning bush as we walk to the shops. God doesn't normally operate this way. I'm not saying that He won't appear to you in some spiritual form, so don't give up believing, but it's not the norm for Christians to experience God as the characters in the Bible did.

The reason I want to explain how God operates is because I believe in this modern age people expect everything to be instant and when God doesn't seem to be operating according to "the rules", people get disillusioned. It's very hard when we hear testimonies from other Christians, when they stand up and reveal how much God has done for them this week, when they testify how the Word was on fire and the Spirit moved them to tears. We are naturally glad for them and we praise the Lord for all He has done for them, but in the back of our minds we wonder why God isn't operating in our own lives in the same way.

The truth is God is working in your life as much as the person who stood up and gave a great testimony, but if we don't understand how God operates then we will miss the little tell-tale signs that reveal Him. In our pride we often expect that God should reveal Himself by sending one of His angels, but this is not His way. He is not into building up our ego. God's way is very different to what we expect. He is only interested in us having a real experience. So, through the Word, He will only reveal a small portion at a time. He gives us small seeds so that we can grow into the experience of that truth. If as Christians we are expecting God to reveal Himself in a big flash then we will be very disappointed because it probably won't happen. And whilst we are looking in the wrong place we will be missing the small voice of the Lord that is trying to be heard, that is trying to reveal the tiny little seed that we need right now to grow in Him.

Many times in the Bible a garden is used to portray a spiritual truth. Romans 1v20 informs us that the invisible aspects of God can be seen in the natural world around us. Matthew 13v31-32: In these two verses we are told about the power of the mustard seed which, according to scripture, is the least of all seeds yet it grows into the most fantastic herb and also becomes a tree. This story and many others like it give us an insight into how God's Word grows within us.

It's important as Christians that we read the Word of God because this is our spiritual food. It's the Word of God that will transform us into His likeness. When we read God's Word we are receiving seeds of truth. They are being planted within us and just like in the natural world when seeds are being sown they are being placed underground in our unconscious. In the natural world these seeds are placed under the soil. They are placed into darkness and we can't see them so we don't really know if they are growing and maturing. Just as the farmer has to trust the laws of nature, we too have to put our faith in God that beneath the surface they are actually growing. Having sown the seeds, the farmer has to wait for the tiny plants to reveal themselves later on in the year. They don't reveal themselves instantly. It may take months for the seeds to grow, but eventually they will surface and grow into whatever the farmer has planted. Whilst our spiritual seeds are hidden in darkness it may seem like God isn't interested, but gradually this new life will begin to expose itself and it's the most wonderful experience that we can have.

Having watched the Chelsea flower show on TV recently I gained a little insight into how God builds our spiritual garden. Those who visit the show through the week when it's on only see the finished article i.e. the wonderful gardens that are on show. But those of us who watch the program on TV see behind the scenes. We see all the work involved in getting the bulbs, plants and garden features just right so that the public can walk in the garden and take in the wonderful sights and aromas that it offers. God is working behind the scenes in our garden. He's watering the seeds, He's ploughing the land, and He's making everything just right so that one day our garden is like the one in the Song of Solomon where our Lord can come and walk, taking in the aroma of our nature. Until that time our garden is like a muddy field. There is plenty of new life stirring under the soil but it's not yet a place where God can come and walk.

For this garden to come to fruition we have to grow and mature and we have to trust God over its development. When Abraham received God's Word it must have been a wonderful experience. He must have felt so special, but how did he feel when God wasn't revealing Himself? Did he feel that God had left him or did he believe that God was working behind the scenes? He may have been surprised at the length of time in between each visit. He may have wondered every morning if this would be the day when the Lord would visit him again, and maybe he was disappointed when God didn't speak to him. The truth is that Abraham never knew when God was going to invade his life, but he was always ready for when that day came. He always believed that God was with him and leading him to the place where he should be. We too are called to have the same faith as Abraham, trusting that the Spirit will lead and guide us in everything that we do.

I wonder what Abraham was thinking when he looked back over His life. Would he have wished for more? I don't suppose we will ever know what he was thinking about, but I've got a sneaky feeling that God was somewhere in his thoughts. His journey was definitely one to remember. It was a long, hard road that he had to walk. He was tested to the limit to see how faithful he would be. His journey began when he was back in his home land of Ur of the Chaldees. He came to Haran with his family. But when his father died his call was renewed and he was asked to leave his country and his father's house, and he was to travel to a place that God would show him.

We are the descendants of Abraham and we too are called to the Promised Land. Our walk, just like his, will be a difficult one. We will be tested just as he was. Abraham and Sarah must have thought that God's promise could never happen, which is why Sarah laughed when the promise was given, but God kept His Word and against all the odds Isaac was born just as the angels had predicted. We have to believe in our hearts that anything is possible when God is involved.

Reaching the heights where God dwells might seem like an awesome thing to do, especially after reading how God manifested Himself to the characters in the Bible and how He interacted with them in a special way. If we have been inspired to follow in their footsteps and we have decided to walk wherever God leads, then it's important that we understand the difficulties that will be involved on our journey. We can be misled into believing that it will be straight forward. After all, the life of Moses was condensed into a few chapters. It didn't seem to take him long before he was chatting with God and was holding his rod up to part the Red

Sea. It all sounds so easy when we see it written down in black and white. What we fail to grasp is all the anguish and pain Moses went through, the inner turmoil that he faced, all the decisions that he had to make and all the obstacles that he had to overcome. It's important for us to recognise that our personal journey will not always be an easy one. There will be obstacles along the way, mental physical and spiritual, that will raise issues that could, if you let them, stop you from fulfilling your call from God.

Abraham was first called to journey to Canaan when his father was alive but they stopped at a place called Haran. Whilst they dwelt in this land his father Terah died. At this point, Abraham was under his father's headship because he was the head of his household, so Abraham had to obey what his father commanded. In Hebrew the name Terah means 'delay'. There will be a lot of situations that come along to try to delay us in our quest. Many are genuine reasons and here it was Abraham's family that stopped him. Family and friends can be a big hindrance, especially because we love them so much and we don't want to hurt their feelings. They say we don't mind you being a Christian but don't take it too far, and they try to make us compromise our faith.

From past experience I can assure you that your journey will probably not be smooth. There will be many obstacles in the way that will try to stop you. The only advice that I can give is when you are delayed, as Abraham was, you still must be faithful in whatever situation you find yourself. Put your trust in God because one day the delay will be removed (if not physically, then its hold over you) and God will renew His calling to you.

If we believe that God is going to achieve the impossible within our lives then we have to accept the path that He asked us to walk. God asks us to walk the path that is right for us, which means that it might be totally different from your best friend who goes to the same church. The reason that your path will be different is because God knows what is in your heart and He knows that your hang-ups are different from your friend's. The only way He can make you realise that your inner nature is corrupt and tainted with sin is if you walk the path that is specifically designed for you.

Your best friend might go to the pub and have a few

drinks but you feel in your heart that you should give up alcohol but, because it has always been a part of your life, you find it very hard to do so. You are not sure why God wants you to give up drinking, but you believe that He knows best, and yet still you wonder why your friend doesn't have the same conviction. The answer lies in our unconscious. God knows that if we have a drink then our unconscious will open up and it will expose areas that we can't control e.g. anger, hate or lust. When these energies are exposed then they can do our Christian walk a lot of damage. God might also be showing you that you use drink as a way to escape your problems. There will be a reason behind why you feel that drink shouldn't be a part of your life, but your friend doesn't have the same problems as you and so God doesn't need to deal with that area in their life.

If we love the Lord and we want to know more of Him daily, then we should never think that we know it all or that we have everything that there is to have from God. If we sit back and say that we have experienced everything and no one can tell us anything more about God, then our vision of Him is too small. It shows that we have not dealt with our inner pride. However great our experience, we have to believe that there is always more because we are dealing with the Almighty Living God. The beauty of a relationship with God is that every day can be a new loving union where we can grow into His nature and walk by His side for eternity.

The End

www.ingramcontent.com/pod-product-compliance
Lightning Source LLC
Chambersburg PA
CBHW071418150726
48000CB00001B/380